WHEN GODS COLLIDE

An unbeliever's pilgrimage along
India's Coromandel Coast

KATE JAMES

hardie grant books

Published in 2012 by Hardie Grant Books

Hardie Grant Books (Australia)
Ground Floor, Building 1
658 Church Street
Richmond, Victoria 3121
www.hardiegrant.com.au

Hardie Grant Books (UK)
Dudley House, North Suite
34–35 Southampton Street
London WC2E 7HF
www.hardiegrant.co.uk

National Library of Australia Cataloguing-in-Publication Data:

James, Kate (Katherine Muriel), 1972–
    When Gods collide : an unbeliever's pilgrimage along India's
    Coromandel Coast / Kate James.
    ISBN: 9781742701189 (pbk.)
    James, Kate (Katherine Muriel), 1972 – Childhood and youth.
    James, Kate (Katherine Muriel), 1972 – Travel.
    Missionaries – India.
    India – Religious life and customs.
915.48

Cover and text design by Peter Daniel
Cover image Getty Images
Typesetting by Kirby Jones
Typeset in ITC New Baskerville Std 11/18pt
Printed and bound in Australia by Griffin Press

'Because He Lives' by Bill and Gloria Gaither. Printed with permission from Word Group Australia.
'Why Worry When You Can Pray' © 1949 John W Peterson Music Company. All rights reserved. Used by permission.
'Tree Song' by Ken Medema. © Word Music LLC. Licensed courtesy CopyCare Pacific.
All biblical quotes © New International Version.

For Chris

About the author

Kate James was born in Melbourne in 1972 and spent most of the 1980s in south India. She has worked as a journalist, editor and guidebook author. Her first book, *Women of the Gobi*, was published in 2006. She lives in Melbourne with her partner and dogs.

CONTENTS

Author's note

A few—just a few—of the names in this book have been changed at the request of the people whom I have written about.

In 2010, the state of Orissa was renamed Odisha, and the local language is now officially called Odia rather than Oriya. I have stuck with the older names, which were used throughout Graham Staines's lifetime and are still more commonly used on the ground.

This project has been assisted by the Australian government through the Australia Council for the Arts, its arts funding and advisory body.

PROLOGUE

The day I heard the news about Graham Staines, I spent the evening sitting on a rug on the floor, up close to the television, hugging my knees to my chest. I watched the Channel Nine news at six o'clock, the SBS news at six-thirty and the ABC news at seven. The images I remember are of a tall white-blonde woman wearing a sari and talking about forgiveness, and a crowded cemetery in bright sunshine where the woman and her teenage daughter stood in front of three fresh graves and didn't cry, though the people in the crowd around them were sobbing loudly. But they sang, unaccompanied:

And then one day I'll cross the river,
I'll fight life's final war with pain.
And then as death gives way to victory,
I'll see the lights of glory and I'll know He lives.

'That was my nana's favourite song,' I said to my housemate Eddy, who had been quietly sitting behind me on the couch for all three news cycles, watching out for me because he had seen me crying. 'She had Alzheimer's disease and she could hardly play the piano any more, but she'd pick out that song note by note and sing along.'

It was January 1999, and I was living in a run-down shared house owned by a Christian community in Melbourne that had been founded by left-leaning Jesus People types in the 1970s. I worked a few doors up the street, in a rented church hall that served as the office for the community's magazine. I wrote news stories, proofread letters to the editor, solicited reviews for contemporary Christian music albums and, once a day, dialled up to the new internet connection that shrieked and pinged before downloading the magazine's emails.

From the front windows of the shared house I could see pretty, green St James Park across the road, but on the inside the place was badly decorated, or rather not decorated, by the three young men who lived there with me. The bare walls and grotty surfaces had become depressing, and I had started hanging floaty curtains and painting kitchen cupboards and tossing Indian bedspreads over op-shop armchairs.

When I'd answered the phone, the sky outside over the park had been bright-blue and cloudless. My father had asked, 'Have you heard about the Staineses?'

I had been putting a colourful rag rug down on the floor in the living room, a space taken up mainly by a television and a slippery grey vinyl couch that had repelled all attempts at covering it with throw-blankets and cushions. The three boys would squish on the couch together to watch *South Park*, and sometimes the twelve-year-old from downstairs would sneak up and join them. His mother would have been horrified.

What we learned from the news reports that evening was that Graham Staines, an Australian missionary in Orissa, east India, had been murdered, along with his ten-year-old and six-year-old sons, by what was described as a 'Hindu mob'. Graham, Philip and Timothy had been sleeping in a jeep while they attended a Bible camp in a small jungle village called Manoharpur, and it had been set alight; when they had tried to escape they'd been stabbed with trishuls— metal tridents said to have been wielded by the Hindu god Shiva. Their bodies had been taken back to the town of Baripada, where the Staines family lived and Graham ran a leprosy mission, and a funeral had been held. Graham's wife, Gladys, had talked to the news media with her daughter, Esther, by her side. She told them that she had forgiven the killers. She had spoken without discernible emotion.

The initial horror and sadness that anyone might have felt was compounded because I had known the Staines family, a little. Esther and Philip had attended the same missionary school in India where my family and I had lived in the 1980s, and where my parents had been teachers. I had met Gladys, Esther and Philip in 1997 when I returned to the school to teach for a couple of months. *Little Philip*, I kept thinking.

I don't remember whether the news reports used the term 'Hindu fundamentalists', but it was suggested that the mob who had attacked the Staineses had objected to missionary activities being carried out. 'It's not what happens in India,' I said, turning round to speak to Eddy again. 'People are so tolerant about other faiths.'

But it had happened. When I spoke to my parents about the attacks, they didn't speculate as to why. They spoke only about Gladys, and their hope that she was being supported by other missionaries and local Christians.

My parents were still close to many missionary families and ran mission support programs at their church in Melbourne. 'These are our people,' my mother said to me.

When I took the magazine job in Melbourne, which led to the cheap room, I had recently returned to Australia after a year travelling overseas, which had included the time spent teaching in India. I'd hoped to have some kind of epiphany while I was travelling, in which I either became happily reconciled to being a Christian in spite of my almost complete lack of faith, or found a way to get out of the whole scene without upsetting my family, who were all dedicated Christians. The epiphany had not transpired, and the magazine had provided an opportunity to be around Christians whose politics, at least, I was comfortable with. Once a week, after work, I talked to a psychologist; if I couldn't see visions, I thought, I'd have to see a professional.

A few days after Graham, Philip and Timothy were killed, I walked into the psychologist's office.

She looked up at me and laughed. 'I was thinking of you in the car on the way here,' she said. 'That song came on the radio, you know—"I'm free to do what I want"—and I was singing along, and I started thinking, wouldn't it be great if Kate could sing that?'

She knew that I didn't feel free. I carried my lack of faith with me like a burden that I wasn't allowed to put down. My whole life, my family and friends and job, were tied to evangelical Christianity. I didn't know how to get away.

I had told the psychologist that I envied my friends who came from Catholic or Hindu backgrounds. In their traditions, you could still call yourself a Catholic, or a Hindu, and be a part of that community, without believing in the literal truth of all its myths, or following all the rules.

But evangelical Christians don't think that way. You're in, or you're out—you play hard or you go home. There's no middle ground. They believe—to differing degrees—

in the literal truth of the Bible as the word of God, and
their understanding of the Bible is that people who don't
repent of their sins and accept that Jesus died on the cross
for them and rose again will go to hell. Some of them are
shyer than others about saying it that plainly, preferring
to focus on God's love, and some will interpret 'hell'
more literally than others, but that's what it appeared to
me to boil down to when I was growing up.

The psychologist was working out of a Christian
counselling centre, but she had in fact been urging me
to get away from the Christians ('for now, at least') ever
since I had first told her my story.

'I'm not free,' I said. 'These are my people.'

From 1980 to 1987, my family and I lived in Ooty,
south India, where my parents were teachers at Hebron
School, the same international boarding school that
Graham and Gladys Staines's older children were sent
to a decade later.

I've read articles by sociologists about so-called
'third culture kids'—people like me and Esther
Staines—who have grown up in the space between
the cultures of their parents and the countries where
they lived as children, never really fitting in with either.
Their defining characteristic seems to be an inability to
answer when someone asks them where they're from.
Because they don't have a good sense of where their
physical home is, the 'third culture' isn't tied to a place,

but to the people who share their background, and their sense of displacement.

It's clear to me now that this is one of the reasons it was so hard for me to reject Christianity. (My brother—an Australian who had lived at a British school in India—married a Ugandan-born British girl who had lived in Borneo and attended an American school in the Philippines. They had a lot in common.)

At the time I lived there, Hebron was my whole world. I didn't remember Australia very well. The culture at Hebron wasn't Indian or Australian, but it was thoroughly evangelical. Prayers and Bible readings and hymns were constants. I was a good kid, and I believed sincerely that Jesus had given his life for me, because that's what I was told. I wasn't much one for questioning received truths.

When I was a teenager, not long before my family left India, Hebron School went through what many people called a 'spiritual revival'. Groups of staff and students met together to pray and started to receive what Christians term the 'gifts of the Holy Spirit'—speaking in tongues, giving words of prophecy—as well as crying, laughing and singing 'in the Spirit'. There were a few conversions of students from Hindu and non-religious backgrounds, but most of the kids swept up in the revival were from Christian families.

I was right in the thick of the revival. At church, and in more informal meetings in the school chapel, I would sing along with the emotional songs about loving Jesus and raise my hands in the air and feel a wave of God's love, or adrenaline, or something, wash over me. We laid hands on each other, and I would cry and cry in what I can see now was a kind of adolescent hysteria. I couldn't understand why a few of the students—and, even worse, a few of the teachers—didn't get involved. Why wouldn't you want to receive the blessings and joy of the Lord?

Some of my former classmates who were not involved have told me since that this phase put them off Christianity, and religion in general, for life. They felt excluded. Others, who were involved, are now as embarrassed about it as I am. There are others who would say that the revival was a wonderful time that marked the start of their Christian walk: judging by their posts on Facebook, most of my old school friends are still enthusiastic Christians.

When I was a little older I decided that Christianity shouldn't be about emotion. It was fine to enjoy a good sing and hand-wave in church, but in the end we followed Jesus because what he said was true. In fact, after I read CS Lewis's *Mere Christianity* when I was sixteen, I believed that Christianity had been logically proved to be true.

And then I grew older again, studied philosophy and read a lot of books by people who weren't CS Lewis. I met some good and smart people who weren't Christians. I saw Christians behaving badly towards other people then claiming they had repented and been forgiven, which seemed an unfair 'get out of jail free' move to me.

In the end, I came to believe that I'm simply not religious, and I don't just mean that I don't practise any particular religion: I don't actually believe in the nebulous idea of 'spirituality'. I suspect that most people use the word to describe a calm or introspective or trance-like state, and that certain atmospheres are conducive to that. The euphoria I felt during the school 'revival' could have been described as spiritual, as could the way I have felt at some non-Christian religious sites as an adult. But I have become suspicious of religious environments that try to induce that kind of feeling. I think it's a con.

For all these reasons and many more I stopped believing, and eventually, a few weeks after the Staines murders, I actually came clean about it to the people I loved, and still love. There was no blinding-light revelation that pushed me to this; I just realised that pretending to be a Christian was a heavier burden than I was capable of carrying.

When I told my family, they were disappointed, but they gave me far more understanding and support than I thought I deserved at the time, for which I was grateful. I resigned from the Christian magazine and left the shared house and moved away from Melbourne. I ended up staying away for two years.

I started out my non-Christian journey as an apologetic agnostic, but over the next ten years I turned into an atheist. I lost some sympathy for my people; I wasn't even sure if they were my people any more. But during those ten years every time I heard news of Gladys and Esther Staines, or reports about the murder investigation, I thought about the sunny cemetery and the three graves and felt a sadness out of all proportion. I dealt with this by shouting at the television or newspaper, or by arguing with anyone unwise enough to talk about the case in front of me.

Depending on who I was talking to, I defended Hinduism. Every time I heard phrases like 'Hindu mob' and 'Hindu fundamentalists', I thought about Chellarams department store in Ooty, where a picture of Jesus hung on the wall next to Lakshmi, the Hindu goddess of wealth, both of which were freshly garlanded every morning. 'It's the most tolerant, syncretistic religion in the world,' I would say to people. In fact, I was ashamed of how little I knew about Hinduism, after all the years I had lived in India. 'Hindu fundamentalism is about politics, not religious belief,' I would go on, in spite of this. 'This would've been about local issues, about class and caste and power, not religion. Maybe untouchables who became Christians stopped kowtowing to high-caste landlords.' But I also wanted to defend Christian missionaries, and, more specifically, these ones. I had known Graham Staines's family a little, and liked them, and I wanted to feel that Graham had been a force for good in the world. Why was that so important to me? It's a good question. I still wanted to defend the missionaries, who had been my people, but I also wanted to create meaning out of suffering. In spite of myself, I realised that this was a very religious impulse.

Ten years after Graham Staines and his sons were killed, I returned to India. It wasn't the first time I'd been back since I lived there, or even the first time since the deaths, but it was the first time that I had consciously thought of my travel as a kind of pilgrimage. I intended to talk to people in India about Graham, to meet Christians and Hindus and even a few atheists, to go to Baripada to see for myself the leprosy mission and the three graves in the walled cemetery. I hoped to get a better feel for why Graham had died, and how religious sentiment was changing in India.

But first, I was going home to Ooty.

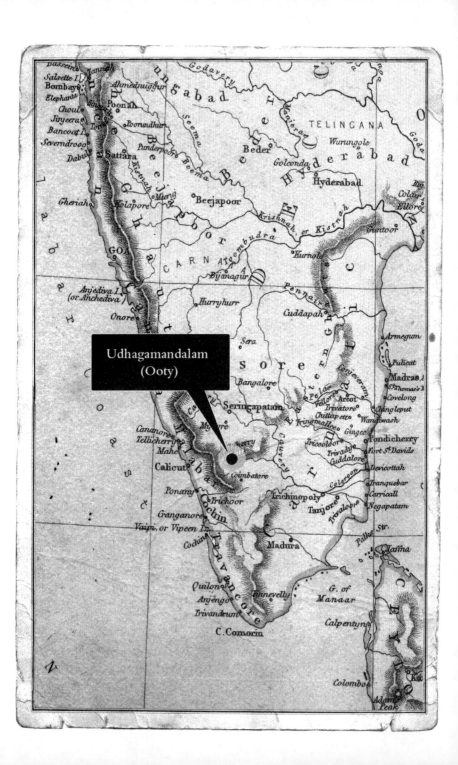

Udhagamandalam
(Ooty)

1

OOTY

I flew out of Melbourne on 12 February 2009, five days after Black Saturday, when 173 people died in bushfires around the state of Victoria, many of them just a few kilometres from the city. The previous summer, a few fires had burned in rural areas outside Melbourne, and the smell of smoke and even tiny pieces of ash had made their way into my suburban front yard. But the winds must have blown in a different direction on Black Saturday, because when I'd stepped outside on that day I hadn't been able to smell anything except the native jasmine. The city had been brightly sunny and still. Yet the news reports on television had talked about walls of fire roaring across the state, and journalists had kept using the phrase 'mounting death toll'.

In the departure lounge at Tullamarine Airport I listened to Can on my iPod and looked out the window at the grey sky. A woman carrying a pile of clipboards tapped me on the shoulder, so I pulled my earplugs out, and she asked if I would fill in a survey that rated how happy I was with the service at the airport. Tullamarine was, as usual, quiet and clean, and the staff had been as helpful and efficient as any I'd seen outside Germany. The last question on the survey asked what my worst experience had been; I wrote, 'Forced to turn off iPod and fill in survey.'

On the plane, air hostesses smiled and offered hot towels and orange juice and newspapers. The fires were still burning. The papers were filled with stories about children suffocating on smoke, elderly couples incinerated while trapped in their cars, and family pets left behind to die. I looked at the front page, then put the paper in the seat pocket and closed my eyes. I didn't want to think about the very last moments. I imagined people huddled together on bedroom floors, inside cars, coughing, and then the pictures flickered and disappeared like an old movie reel. I knew what I was doing. For ten years I'd been picturing the mob marching across the field to Manoharpur with flaming torches, then standing, shouting, around the Staineses' jeep, rocking it, and as I'd focused on the back window and seen three indistinct figures inside, I'd stopped imagining the scene. I didn't want to see their faces.

In Singapore I had five hours to wait before I caught my connecting flight to Coimbatore, the closest airport to Ooty. I walked in circles around the terminals, past what seemed to be the same recurring duty-free watch and liquor shops, until I found the rooftop swimming pool. A British family was splashing about, and some Scandinavian girls in bikinis were sitting at the bar. I swam laps without stopping, forcing the children out of my path, enjoying stretching my body after being cramped on the plane. Australians take swimming more seriously than anyone else, I think. I remember seeing an Australian film director on television accepting her statuette at an international awards show and apologising for the swimming-goggle marks around her eyes—she had been thrashing out laps in her hotel pool and lost track of time.

Ten hours later, at night at Coimbatore Airport, I stood in the customs queue, watching four young Americans who were ahead of me. The woman wore a t-shirt with the slogan 'DARE to resist drugs and violence'. She sat on her bag and stared at the floor. Sweat ran down her face. The oldest guy had a soul patch and tattoos, and his t-shirt read 'Isaiah 53:4–5' on the front and 'Body piercing changed my life' on the back. (When I was next at a computer I looked up the Bible verse. In the New International Version it reads, 'But he was pierced for our transgressions, he was crushed for our iniquities; the punishment that brought us peace was upon him, and by his wounds we are healed.')

I planned that when we got outside I would ask the Americans where they were staying and suggest sharing a taxi into town. But when we walked past the security guards and into the humidity and diesel-fume smells and taxi touts, a group of neatly dressed Indian men ran towards the Americans with strings of jasmine and marigolds.

'Pastor, pastor, oh welcome, pastor,' they said to Soul Patch.

'Well, hey there, guys,' he said, leaning forward so they could garland him.

I caught my own taxi into Coimbatore.

In the morning I walked across the street from the hotel to a shack selling dosai and idli vada, typical south Indian breakfast food made with various forms of steamed and fried chickpea flour and served with sambar and coconut chutney. When my family first returned from India to Australia, in 1987, I used to have dreams about this kind of food. Back then, the only Indian restaurants in Melbourne sold generic north Indian curries, rich and meat-heavy, and my mother never learned to cook these types of snacks. These days, in Melbourne I can walk from my house up to Preston Market and buy a dosa, and it will taste great, and I'll be content as long as I don't convert the cost of the dosai from dollars into rupees. But being back in India, eating dosai and idli off a banana leaf in a side street with a view of goats eating tattered film posters off a wall … this really made me happy.

I was actually a little bit high on a combination of jet lag, chutney and coming home.

I booked a taxi to take me on the three-hour drive up over two thousand metres into the Nilgiri Hills to Ooty, and as we set off I wound down the window and let the hot wind tangle my hair. I looked out at stray dogs and open drains and banana trees and huge billboards of film star Mithun Chakroborthy advertising steel rods. Rows of brightly painted shops and stalls with hand-lettered signs line the Ooty road: we drove past 'suitings and shirtings', pharmacies, computer repair centres and stalls with cooking pots of every size.

The road twists up the hill in hairpin bends, through vegetation that changes slowly from palms and paddy fields to overgrown jungle and then tea plantations and stands of eucalyptus and cypress trees, past the settlements of Aravankadu and Ketti, and through small, familiar hamlets that I hadn't consciously thought about for twenty years. But they had appeared in my dreams, like the dosai. The rock wall at the side of the road, the only thing between vehicles and the sheer drop into the jungle, has only ever been about knee-high, hardly an impediment to a drunk truck driver in a reckless mood, and now it is crumbling away in places. It still provides a good walkway for the little grey monkeys, though. Every time we travelled this road in the 1980s, I imagined that, at some stage, the bus would career over the edge of the cliff and we would plunge into Ketti Valley. I pictured the fall—with everyone screaming 'Aaaah' like in a cartoon—but not the landing.

We passed through Wellington, a town set around a military base, and drove past the gunpowder factory, where a garlanded statue of the famously pacifist Mahatma Gandhi stands outside the gates. My dad used to point out the statue and chuckle at the irony every time we went past. As we continued to climb, I looked down the valley at the town, trying to locate the military house where I once stayed.

When I was about eleven years old, I had a friend called Sara who lived in Wellington. She was what Americans call an army brat: her father had been posted there from the United States for six months, maybe a year—plenty of time for a kid to forge an intense friendship and have her heart broken when the next move to the other side of the world was announced. My friends were always disappearing, and we didn't have Facebook back then.

Sara once invited me to stay at her family's place for a weekend. I was overawed by how American-looking it was. They had a fridge and a television, and everything was clean and shiny, and they ate foods that I'd never seen in India.

'We had asparagus, out of a tin,' I told my mother.

She laughed. 'Did you hear that, Bill? Asparagus out of a tin!'

My mother told me the story, again, of the naive American missionaries who had transported a washing machine to a remote village on the back of a bullock cart only to discover there was no electricity there. She seemed a bit disappointed at my enthusiasm for *things* and perhaps regretted letting me see how the other half lived.

One day, Sara and I were rollerskating on the roof of the junior school block and she asked, out of nowhere, 'So are you all religious like everyone else around here?'

I stiffened and said 'Yes,' and we didn't talk about it again.

I was shocked that she even needed to ask, and that she had phrased it that way—'all religious'—which meant that she obviously didn't believe in Jesus, because if she did she wouldn't talk about it as 'religion'. Instead, she would say that she had accepted Jesus as her saviour. 'Religion', I'd been told many times, was about ritual and dryness, what people of other faiths and nominal Christians practised. But real Christianity was alive. You could see it, the teachers said to each other, in the joy and changed lives of the Hindu and Muslim students who came to know the Lord.

Just past Wellington, the driver pulled over at a roadside stall and insisted on buying me a cup of tea. In the

years since I lived in south India, the chai wallahs have
stopped using the cloudy, heavy glasses I remember,
and instead they hand out tiny, flimsy plastic cups that
people throw on the ground when they're finished. The
goats can't eat them, though not through want of trying,
and the cups pile up around the stalls. From what
I've seen, the cups are eventually swept into rubbish
piles that are set alight, sending out acrid smoke and
occasional flames of unexpected colours.

The tea was fantastic, though: hot, strong and sweet,
like a shot of espresso.

'What is your country?' the taxi driver asked me.
When I told him, he smiled and said, 'You play the
cricket! Ricky Ponting!'

We threw our cups on the ground and drove on,
past more bright-green tea plantations, and then into
Ooty, which was dirtier and more traffic-filled than I
remembered, with lots of new, shoddy-looking concrete
buildings. But somehow it still seemed exactly the same.

We drove through the town, past Charing Cross and
the Gandhi statue and the Assembly Rooms Cinema and
the Tibetan woollens stalls and up the steep driveway of
the school. The taxi stopped right in front of the flat
where my family used to live. I could have peeked into
my old bedroom window, but instead I paid the driver,
slung my bag over my shoulder and walked a few steps
across the tarmac to the new school hall. I read the
plaque attached to the front wall: 'The Graham Staines

Memorial Hall. In memory of Graham, Philip and Timothy Staines, deceased 23rd January 1999. Loved and valued members of the Hebron School family. Re-dedication on Sunday 15th December 2008 by Gladys (parent) and Esther (class of 2004) Staines. *Deo Supremo.* "I am making everything new!" (Revelation 21:5).' I took a photo and turned back to the whitewashed block of flats where I used to live.

When we lived there, our flat was decorated with reminders that we were Australian. Our nationality was easier for me to forget than for my parents, who used to dream about lamb chops and fish-and-chip-shop dim sims. My mother was an art teacher, and she had made a fair stab at copying one of Arthur Boyd's Shoalhaven paintings, the result of which was hung over the fireplace. A group of missionary-supporting Brethren women in Tasmania who mailed us occasional parcels of instant soup, jelly crystals and dried apricots once sent us a tablecloth decorated with pictures of Australian animals. Occasionally, at breakfast, my father would goad me and my brother, Jack, into an argument by telling us how the animal under his plate was superior to all the others.

'The noble wombat, so humble, yet strong and hard-working,' he would muse, then he would look to see which animals we had in front of us. 'Not like that showy black swan, black like the sin in man's heart.'

We knew from his tone that he was joking with us. This was not the way he usually talked about Christian things.

'Oh no, the black swan has a beauty that reflects its inner goodness,' I would say, once I'd got the hang of the game.

The next day, after my mother had shaken the toast crumbs off the tablecloth and put it back in a different position, my father would praise the brave kangaroo and mock the ugly old wombat. At the time I thought he was funny.

Many years later, I reminded my mother of the breakfast arguments, reflecting that teaching children that you could argue anything was a confusing lesson coming from a man who read the Bible every night and believed in absolute truth. 'It might explain some of my problems,' I said jokingly.

A few months later I visited my parents and noticed the native Australian animals tablecloth folded up on a chair by the front door.

'I thought you left that in India,' I said.

'It's not the same one,' my mother said. 'I found that one at an op shop. After what you said, I thought you might like to show it to your psychologist.'

She was mainly joking, I think.

I took the tablecloth home. It led to me sharing my partner, Chris's, long-standing interest in old-fashioned Australiana, which has since blossomed into something of a passion. We recently upgraded from a sixty-spoon to a hundred-spoon Australia-shaped ornamental teaspoon rack, with a little three-spoon Tasmania suspended on a wire underneath. These days, my parents own a collection of Indian woodblock tablecloths featuring paisley and elephant designs, and on the wall over the dining table is my mother's painting of eucalyptus trees silhouetted against the evening sky in Ooty.

I walked up the path through the garden to the Hebron staffroom, where plates of biscuits and huge urns of tea were laid out for morning tea. Only a few teachers remembered my family, but everyone was keen to chat when they heard I was a former staff kid. I asked people about the new hall and the dedication to Graham and the boys. I was told that Gladys and Esther Staines had flown out from Australia, where they were now living, to visit the leprosy mission in Orissa, and had come to Ooty to unveil the plaque. It had been a low-key event: they had visited during the school holidays, so only a few people attended the ceremony.

I could easily picture Gladys and Esther, distinctively tall, blonde and straight-backed, Gladys in her sari and Esther wearing a salwar kameez, the way they had appeared in every photo I'd seen of them over the previous ten years. I had read articles about Gladys and had seen occasional YouTube clips of her talking to journalists or addressing meetings around the world. She was not a charismatic speaker, but she was famous in evangelical circles as the widow of a martyr, and she seemed to go wherever she was invited, reading sometimes from her notes, preaching the same message: that God had a plan, and that we had to forgive. She used the same words—'when my family was killed'—every time she needed to refer to the death of her husband and boys. I had imagined her choosing the phrase and sticking with it, the words losing their impact with every repetition.

One teacher said that the simple unveiling ceremony had been very different from what she described as the 'circus' surrounding the official opening of the hall during the school term. The ribbon at that event had been cut by the school's most famous former student, a millionaire beer magnate who had recently been admitted to Britain's House of Lords. 'There was a convoy of cars, and bodyguards, and all the kids had to listen to him talk about his schooldays, and journalists came,' she said.

'He wasn't even a Christian,' someone else added. 'Here we were making a big fuss of him, and he talked in his speeches about how Hebron was such a special place and he just didn't know what it was that made it special, and I thought'—and here the teacher put on a sarcastic voice—'Yes, I wonder what it is.' Clearly, the teacher thought that its Christian ethos was what made the school special.

I didn't know what to say. I smiled and nodded.

Later, I walked across town with one of the dormitory mothers; we were heading to the school's girls hostel, where I was going to spend a couple of nights. Liz was from New Zealand and had two children. 'Are you glad you grew up here?' she asked. 'Do you think it was good for you?'

I told her that when I was younger I would have answered with an unqualified yes. While at the school I had made friends from all over the world. I had been given a lot of physical freedom and could roam around the hills with the other staff kids. I'd even travelled alone on an overnight bus from Bangalore to Ooty when I was fourteen years old; I've never forgotten the exhilaration I felt walking home by myself from the bus stand early that morning, while the town was still quiet and dark and cold, with the frost crunching under my sneakers as I crossed Breeks Field. When I returned to Australia at fifteen, I was independent, knew a lot about international politics and had, in many ways, a much broader picture of the world than most kids of my age.

But in other ways I had been very sheltered. 'We lived in a bit of an expatriate evangelical bubble here,' I told Liz. 'I had no real interaction with an adult who wasn't a Christian until I was well into my teens. If I'd lived in Australia I would have come across people from my own culture who weren't Christians, even if it was only on the TV, you know, and I'd've realised that they weren't all lost, or ignorant, or sad, or in wilful rebellion.'

When I first returned from India to live in Australia, in 1987, I was looking forward to my new life, to eating ice-cream and lamb chops instead of boarding school curry, to buying fashionable clothes instead of dodgy knock-offs from the Ooty tailor, to hearing Duran Duran and U2 on the radio instead of the BBC World Service and to shopping in clean supermarkets instead of smelly markets where people sat on the ground with a pile of guavas or plastic combs or dekshis in front of them.

It was June, the middle of winter, when we landed in Melbourne. I shivered for the first few days because I didn't even own a coat, and when my mother bought me a puffy purple jacket at Louis' Economy Shop in Box Hill it didn't look the same as the coats the other girls were wearing. We stayed with my grandparents in Mooroolbark; all around the house the trees had dropped their leaves on the ground, and the sky was always grey.

I've never known grief like I experienced in those first months. I felt as if everyone I cared about had died, or, even worse, as if I had died and all my friends in India were carrying on real life without me. I was sent to a Baptist girls school where nearly everyone was white. I had a stupid accent. In India I had caught buses across the state on my own, but here I didn't know how to buy a train ticket or use a public phone, and I ended up on the Belgrave line instead of the Lilydale line and cried in the toilets when I got off the train at a station I didn't recognise. In India I had been proud of being Australian, but now I realised I wasn't Australian at all. But nor did I feel Indian. I wasn't sure what I was, or where my home was.

Liz and I passed Sait's bike shop, where I used to have my pushbike repaired and which now appeared to be a motorcycle repair and hire stand. Sait had gone up in the world.

Liz asked if I was married, and I told her that I live with my boyfriend, and that made everything clear to her. I was not one of them: an evangelical Christian would not live with someone without being married to them.

We walked up the steep, potholed driveway to the girls hostel. Like everything in Ooty except the horseracing track, the hostel is built on a slope. I could hear music coming out of one of the rooms and laughed when I recognised it as Bonnie Tyler's 'Total Eclipse of the Heart'. When I lived at the hostel, I had played the same song over and over on a Walkman after Jehudi Blom broke up with me, and I figured the song must now be retro cool. A gaggle of teenage girls sat on the grass talking about boys, or possibly Jesus, if my memories were anything to go by.

I stayed with Welsh couple Paul and Angie, dormitory parents at the hostel, who had been working at the school, on and off, for more than twenty-five years, since they were first married. In the 1980s they had travelled with my family on holidays to Pondicherry, and they remembered the day I was baptised in front of the English, Tamil and Badaga congregations at Union Church. We drank Nilgiri tea at the kitchen table and shared family news. Their eldest daughter had finished school at Hebron and was at university in Liverpool, and they hoped she was doing all right.

'She's not street smart,' Paul said. 'And now she's in the halls of residence with all those drunks.'

I asked Paul about changes they'd seen in the country, and he said that urban India had become rapidly pseudo-Westernised over the previous couple of years. 'But as my mother-in-law used to say, it's all fur coat, no knickers,' he added. 'It's all on the surface.'

I told him that I'd heard conflicting reports about changes in Indian society. Some writers said it had become richer and more secular, with a focus on the more tolerant and syncretistic aspects of Hinduism and with just a noisy fringe of fundamentalists. I admitted that's what it looked like to me, on the surface. But other commentators said that the fundamentalists were gaining more and more support and influence; the anti-Christian, anti-Muslim, nationalist Hindu ideology known as Hindutva was being embraced by ordinary Hindus, especially young men who had been left behind in the rush to Westernise. I mentioned the young Pakistani Muslim men who rampaged through Mumbai in 2008, killing scores of people and almost destroying the Taj Mahal Hotel: two sides of a coin.

'There are two Indias,' Paul said, 'and they're moving further apart.' He said that the fundamentalists might be on the fringes, but they were getting noisier. Even here in Ooty, a small town with an international population and no history of communal violence, there had been protests that year against the decadent Western custom of celebrating Valentine's Day.

I laughed, but Paul was serious.

'Courting couples were attacked in the botanical gardens; they shouted at people not to hold hands in public. Big hotels like the Savoy have had special Valentine's dinner dances in the past, but no-one did anything this year.'

After dinner a dozen or so teenage girls knocked on the door and filled up the living room and watched a DVD, a derivative 1997 romantic comedy called *Sliding Doors*, in which the leading man is supposed to be charming and witty because he quotes Monty Python routines in a silly voice. The girls took the film absolutely at face value, booing the villain and offering advice to heroine Gwyneth Paltrow ('Don't listen to him, girl, he's lying!'). Afterwards, I wondered why I'd sat through the whole film (for the second time in my life, to my shame) when I could have been reading in my room. I put it down to jet lag.

The next morning I asked Angie if I could help with anything, and she gave me the girls' underwear to hang on the washing line out the front of the house. She explained that it was too delicate to go to the dhobi wallah and get smacked against rocks, so she did a load in her washing machine every few days. It was the first washing machine I had ever seen in India. I thought about the much-cited and probably apocryphal American washing machine being carried on a bullock cart; this machine had probably come up the hill in a Tata Sumo, which seemed to be the minivan of choice all over India.

I hung out thirty-odd pairs of cotton underpants, each with an embroidered nametag sewn into the waistband, and looked across to the hills on the other side of the valley. I used to stare out at the same view from the upstairs room I shared here with five other girls, where we had fought over which posters from *Smash Hits* magazine to tape to the walls. (I had voted for the dreamy close-up of Morten from A-ha.) I thought about Esther Staines, who had lived here for four years after her father and brothers died, and I imagined her sitting on her bed looking out at the same view, feeling safe.

I spent the rest of the day, and then the next morning, walking around Ooty, retracing the routes where I used to ride my bike. I browsed in Higginbothams Bookshop and bought chocolate at King Star and a dosa at Blue Hills Restaurant, and walked past Union Church and further up the hill to St Stephen's Church. In the early afternoon, on my way to the train station, I visited the silver market, where Mr Mahaveerchand and his jewellery shop looked just the same. He was busy showing gemstones to some young Indian women who were wearing jeans and speaking in English, but he gave me a nod of recognition.

'Which is your god?' he asked one of the women.

'Ganesh,' she said.

'For me also. Then this is the right stone for you,' he said.

When the women left, Mr Mahaveerchand said to me, 'Oh yes, you bought those garnet earrings.' That had been twelve years earlier, on my twenty-fifth birthday.

'You remember?' I laughed, and he smiled and said, 'Yes, because I have now a matching pendant and ring; let me show you.'

Half an hour later, carrying jewellery I hadn't planned to buy, I walked on to the train station to catch the toy train that travels down the hill to Mettupalayam, where I was going to meet the overnight Nilgiri Express to Chennai.

The vegetation changed as we steamed along. At first we passed though tea bushes and eucalyptus stands. There had been no rain for months, Mr Mahaveerchand had told me, and the trees looked dry. I thought about the gum trees around Melbourne, imagining them bursting into flames in the bushfires. As we approached Coonoor I carefully scanned the landscape for monkeys. Ooty is too cold for monkeys to live there comfortably, and when we travelled down the hill when I was a child my father often promised a rupee to the first person to spot a monkey. Coonoor was usually the first place they were seen.

I told the monkey story to the people sitting with me in the tiny compartment. We were in Tamil Nadu, but none of the other travellers were Tamil—the train was mostly for tourists, as it was slower and more expensive than the bus—and we spoke to each other in English. A young couple from Andhra Pradesh were on holiday with their eighteen-month-old daughter, whom they clearly adored, constantly fussing over and petting her. She wore a velvet ribbon in her hair, and dangling gold earrings. I have often seen parents like this and have found it hard to square with articles in the Western media about female children not being wanted in India; yet later in my trip, an Indian doctor assured me that there is a problem across the country with pregnant women having ultrasounds to determine the sex of their child and then aborting females.

The other couple were from Delhi, and they were on their honeymoon. They were in their early twenties, educated, good-looking and well off. The young man said that south India felt like a different country to them. Not many people in the south spoke Hindi, he added, so they could only communicate in English. He and his wife were happy and giggly, obviously thrilled with each other, taking photos of each other leaning precariously out of the train window.

As the sun started to set over the hills, the honey-mooners asked about my travels, and I told them about my interest in Graham Staines. I was surprised that they had never heard of him. Five years earlier, the last time I had travelled in south India, everyone I met had wanted to talk about the deaths, especially when they found out I was Australian. They had told me it was very sad, and that Gladys Staines was inspiring, and, most importantly, that this was not Hinduism: the killers were not Hindus. They were goondas, thugs. The killings had probably been about local politics. India welcomes all religions, they had told me, and I had assured them that yes, I knew this.

The train wound its way down the hills and the sun disappeared. I looked out into the dusk, over the dark patch of jungle below us and across to the lights of Mettupalayam flickering on the plains. The sky was darkened but not yet quite black.

When I was eight years old, travelling down to Mettupalayam by bus with my family, I looked out at the same view, at the same time of the evening, and felt the warm air on my skin. I thought it the most beautiful view I had ever seen. I told myself I would never forget this scene, or the way it made me feel.

A family friend, a bible translator called Ray Valentine, was sitting in front of me, next to his two sons, also looking out across the plains. He didn't turn around, but I thought he was speaking to me. 'It's such a beautiful country,' he said, 'but so lost. So many millions of souls that will die in darkness without the Lord.'

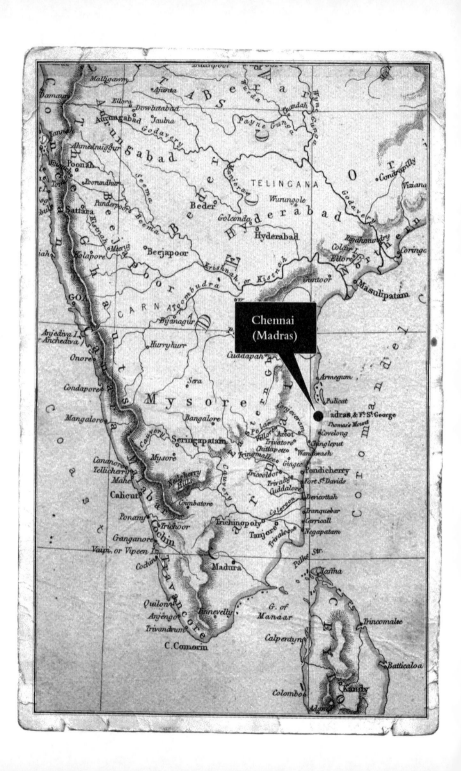

2

CHENNAI

I loved travelling on overnight trains when I was a kid. To reach the top bunk you had to climb a ladder like a Coonoor monkey, and my brother and I would jump up enthusiastically, swinging from the ladder and making monkey noises. Once I was up there I had my own private cubby house, where I could read or just watch the other passengers without having them stare back at me. And I was out of reach of old Indian women who wanted to pinch my cheeks.

For this trip on the Nilgiri Express from Mettupalayam to Chennai I had booked a top bunk and still preferred it for many of the same reasons, though it had been some time since anyone had tried to pinch my cheeks. But I'm built more like elephant god Ganesh than monkey god Hanuman these days, and when you see an elephant climb a narrow ladder into a small, enclosed space, to paraphrase Dr Johnson, the wonder is not that she does it well but that she does it at all. I threw my bag up to the top berth, slipped off my chappals and swung clumsily up the ladder. I was wearing the traditional salwar kameez pants-and-tunic set, and I pictured myself stepping on the hem of my salwar pants and having them fall down in front of everyone—everyone being an elderly man wearing a lungi, and his large wife, who had wisely booked the bottom berth.

I slept badly, as always, alternately being rocked to sleep and sharply woken when we reached a busy station or when the man on the other side of the compartment let out a sudden snore, and each time I woke I felt a crick in my neck from using my lumpy bag as a pillow. I have never had anything stolen from me in all the years I have lived and travelled in India, but I keep my bag close to me all the same.

It was five o'clock and still dark when we pulled in at Chennai Central. I caught an autorickshaw down Periyar EVR High Road, a major thoroughfare named for Tamil Nadu's most famous atheist and arguably one of south India's most important twentieth-century social reformers, described in 1970 by Unesco as 'the Socrates of South East Asia'. I lived in Tamil Nadu for eight years and had never heard of Periyar, but then, we didn't study any Indian history at Hebron. On my most recent visit to the school, I'd been pleased to hear that the Hebron students at least have to learn Hindi these days.

Actually, this last fact would have infuriated EVR Periyar. Of course he wanted to get rid of the British, but the people he really hated were northerners, the Hindi-speaking Indo-Aryans who he said were oppressing the Dravidians of the south. Brahmin-dominated Hinduism and its caste system were parts of the problem, he believed, and he told his poor, lower caste followers that they should consider converting to Islam, Buddhism or Christianity if they thought they'd get a better deal that way. Today, Periyar EVR High Road has the same mix of religious establishments as any Indian city.

We turned in to the driveway of the YWCA, where my family and I spent our very first night in India, in January 1980, when I was seven years old and the city was still called Madras. My only memories of that day are of feeling hot, seeing bullock carts on the road, and the dank, humid smell of the bathroom at the Y.

I've been back to the Y every few years since then. It's an attractive old building in leafy grounds and has the feel of a missionary guesthouse without any of the overt Christian emphasis.

The grounds were still dark and quiet when I arrived, but the lobby light was on. When I reached the front desk, a young French couple were checking in. They had obviously just flown in to Chennai, and they were carrying duty-free bags containing whisky and cigarettes. The girl wore a thin cotton top with no bra.

The television in the lobby was tuned in to a Hindu station. Nobody was watching it. The sound was turned down, but I could see a black stone lingam being anointed over and over with milk, then with turmeric-coloured milk, and then with what looked like oil. Then a priest wearing a saffron robe smeared something that resembled grainy upma, my most hated childhood breakfast, over the stone. Each scene was repeated many times in slow motion, with the milk cascading sensuously over the stone. I wondered just how Christian the Y was these days. But perhaps the television had been switched to a random station and nobody had bothered to change it.

Christians have lived in Chennai for a long time, and legend has it that one of the very first Christians died there. In the weeks after the deaths of Graham Staines and his boys, I heard a lot of Australians say that Christianity was alien and foreign in India, a recent Western import, and every time I read an article or heard an academic opining on the radio I thought about the Saint Thomas Christians. Known also as Nasranis, these Christians have been a distinct ethnic and religious group in south India for almost two thousand years and are said to have been originally converted by the apostle Thomas. They retained a Hindu-style caste system, and high-born families today still claim that their ancestors were baptised by the apostle. For a long time historians thought the legend was just that, though they couldn't deny the existence of a long-established and distinctively Indian form of Christianity in the south. But the Saint Thomas story isn't necessarily untrue: trade between the Middle East and the Malabar Coast flourished in the first century AD, and Roman coins from the era have been found along the Malabar Coast. In 2002, writer William Dalrymple investigated the legend for the BBC and successfully recreated the journey across the Arabian Sea in a fishing boat.

Thomas is said to have landed in Kerala, on the southwest coast, where he lived and preached. He is then supposed to have crossed the country to the Coromandel Coast and lived in the region of Chennai. This is where he fell foul of local Brahmins, who thought Christianity threatened the caste system, and he was killed on a mountaintop outside town, stabbed to death with a lance.

Growing up in evangelical circles, I didn't hear anything about the apostle Thomas's travels, but I heard lots of sermons about his doubt ('Don't be a Doubting Thomas; rest fully on His promise,' we sang in Sunday School.) In the gospel of John, Thomas says that he won't believe that Jesus has risen from the dead until he, Thomas, sticks his finger in the nail-holes in Jesus' hands. He wants some evidence. And Jesus says 'Fair enough' and pretty much waltzes in and shows him his hands and says 'That good enough for ya?' and Thomas says 'Fair cop'. (Actually, he says 'My Lord and my God'.)

Because of the legends, many sites around Chennai have purported links to Saint Thomas. I wonder what the 'show me the evidence' apostle would think of the mishmash of stories, dodgy relics and superstitions that have grown up around him.

I had decided to do a spot of Saint Thomas tourism while I was in town. The receptionist at the Y called a taxi for me. The driver had a fresh pottu on his forehead and a lurid Ganesh surrounded by fibre-optic lights on his dashboard, and he knew the Saint Thomas sites well. He said he would take me first to Chinnamalai, a hillock where Thomas is said to have lived in a cave and preached to the locals. A series of churches and chapels has been built there over the years, but the cave is still a cave.

We drove through a nondescript neighbourhood and down a side street between some houses, and there was Chinnamalai. The name means 'little mount', and it really is little: not so much a mount as a slightly raised mound with low walls around it. I climbed the few stairs past brightly painted life-sized statues of saints outside a new-looking chapel. I was surprised at just how recently constructed everything appeared, but when I looked at the ground I saw seventeenth-century tombstones set into the concrete and exposed to the weather, one bearing Portuguese text and topped with a crude skull and crossbones.

A bearded old man with thick glasses and no teeth pointed me to the smaller chapel, which houses the entrance to Thomas's cave. I made my way past more gaudy statuary and squeezed through a gap in the rock. It wasn't easy; I had to suck in my stomach, and when I got inside the cave I couldn't quite stand up, and I started to feel my heart beat faster. I always forget my tendency towards claustrophobia until I'm in these situations. The last time I'd felt like this was in Turkey, on a tour of an underground city in Cappadocia, where I'd started to shake and had to make a break for the wobbly staircase.

This is just a cave, but all the surfaces are shiny; generations of pilgrims must have run their fingers reverently over the rocks. A wiry young woman was chanting at an altar, and she turned and fixed me with her glittering eye. She spoke no English, but she showed me the supposed sacred footprints and handprints, and rocks where Thomas prayed. She touched each spot and then kissed her fingers, then indicated that I should do the same. She didn't seem the type to put up with disobedience, so I vaguely waved my fingers near my lips and hoped I wouldn't catch pilgrim flu.

After we did the rounds of the extra-sacred patches of cave wall, my guide looked lovingly at me and gave me a big hug, as if I were her sister, as if we had made a wonderful connection in our shared love of Saint Thomas. Then she gestured to the offering box. These are everywhere at the Saint Thomas sites, I discovered, reminding me of nothing so much as Buddhist temples I've visited in China. I felt a bit flustered, as much by claustrophobia as religious pressure, and put a fifty-rupee note in the box (and instantly regretted it). I turned to head out of the cave, but my sister took my arm, made the universal hand symbol for money and pointed to herself, so I grimaced and handed over another note. She tucked it into her sari blouse, and as I squeezed out I could hear her chanting again.

Outside, the bearded man was waiting to walk me to the chapel constructed over the miracle spring that Thomas called forth by smiting the rock. A metal cup on a chain was lowered into a chasm between two rocks by a woman who looked like the twin of my cave sister. She pulled it up again, full of water, and handed it to me to drink.

Oh man.

On 5 January 1980, the day my family first landed in India, my mother saw a tap at the airport labelled 'Drinking water'. She had already been warned not to drink tap water, but the sign reassured her that this must be specially treated water, so she drank it. And she spent the next couple of weeks in bed, sick with giardia.

So this was the very first lesson I learned in India: don't drink the water. Others were don't eat ice-cream (we often heard the story of The Little Girl Who Almost Died After Eating Ice-Cream), don't drink squeezed juice, don't eat salad and don't touch animals. But most of all, don't drink the water; don't even brush your teeth in it. Our immune systems just couldn't handle all those new and unfamiliar bugs.

But at Chinnamalai I knew straightaway that I had to drink the miracle water. No real journey is without risk, or commitment. Just before I left Melbourne I'd read the Indian memoirs of Australian journalist Christopher Kremmer, who had felt obligated, after reporting on religious issues in the country for years, to take his own literal plunge into the filthy holy water of the River Ganges in Varanasi. It seemed to be his metaphor for taking risks and not behaving like an impartial outsider, recognising that no-one is an impartial outsider.

So I took a sip of the miracle water, but I didn't meditate on how God had provided Saint Thomas with a miracle spring. Instead, I pictured my little medical kit with its *Health Advice for Australian Travellers* handbook, and I mentally opened it to the page headed 'Diarrhoea flow chart', which I had thought hilarious when I first saw it, and decided that it would probably be about twenty-four hours until I got sick. I calculated that I had a spare day in my schedule to lie in bed at the Y and vomit.

I gave the book-and-medallion shop a miss and headed down the mound. My driver hastily dropped his cigarette and ground it into the dirt when he saw me coming, and we drove out of town to Periamalai, the 'big mount', known by most people as St Thomas Mount.

The driver spent most of this trip talking on his phone in Tamil. I'd already noticed that everyone, and I mean *everyone*, in India now owns a mobile phone. On streets where traffic seems wildly chaotic by Western standards, it adds a certain piquancy to the adventure to know that all those lorry drivers and rickshaw wallahs are driving one-handed.

Periamalai is more of a hill than the little mount, but it still isn't really a mountain. It is high enough to give expansive views, though: across Chennai from one side of the whitewashed shrine, and over to the international airport from the other. This is supposed to be the site of the apostle's martyrdom. The cave at Chinnamalai contains a small, tunnel-like window said to have miraculously appeared when the apostle's killers arrived; from there he apparently escaped to this spot at Periamalai, where they caught up with him. One wonders what the point of the original miracle was.

We parked partway up the hill, and I walked the rest of the way, past scrubby trees and through a gate with a sign reading 'No jogging or exercises beyond the gate'. I assumed this was to maintain a dignified atmosphere at the shrine, or perhaps to ensure that nobody's legs were shown off in jogging shorts, causing a pilgrim to have inappropriate thoughts. Then I passed a snack bar called Mount Manna, named after the miracle food that God sent from heaven to the Israelites wandering in the desert; the shop was selling ice-creams and bhuja mix, and I decided that this detracted from a sacred atmosphere more than any fitness enthusiast could.

The whole concept of sacred places is hard to fathom when you grow up in a low-church tradition. Like Gladys Staines, my mother's family, and consequently my parents, are members of the Open Brethren, an ecumenical movement that was formed at least partly in reaction against the smells and bells of the Church of England. They have traditionally met in bare old halls and believe that feelings of awe should be evoked by pondering the nature of the Almighty, not by stained-glass windows or soaring music or mummified fingers of saints. There were no places or objects designated as sacred when I was a child; you would take care of a Bible, perhaps, but only in the same way that you would look after any book.

Today I'm grateful for this rational, anti-magic thinking, which balanced some of the other supernatural things I was taught. But while I'm sceptical about sacred sites and relics, I also hate to cause offence, so it's always nerve-racking to be around them because I have no idea how to behave. Am I allowed to turn my back on the altar? Should I take off my shoes? Does it matter if I approach from the left or the right? When, and in which direction, should I bow?

Luckily for me, the Saint Thomas shrine at Periamalai was being renovated when I visited, so all the rules seemed to have been put on hold. In spite of the signs warning pilgrims to remove their shoes and keep silent, labourers ran back and forth in front of the altar in their chappals, balancing bags of concrete on their heads and shouting to each other above the roar of jackhammers. Scaffolding was fixed around the sacred altar, the centrepieces of which are a stone cross apparently carved by Saint Thomas, a portrait of the Virgin Mary painted by Saint Luke and a sliver of Thomas's bone. The cross is supposed to have bled miraculously; the painting looks a lot more Renaissance Italian than first-century Judaic; and the original site of the bone is not specified.

Outside, a stone altar was set against the shrine wall; it obviously belonged inside but had been pushed out during the renovations. Angels and flowers and crosses were carved on it, along with a mermaid wearing a cross-shaped hat. But was she a mermaid? I'd seen similar images on the walls of fifteenth-century temples in Orissa and had been told there that this was the figure of the Nagarani, the Hindu snake goddess. In Kerala, after all, Christians and Hindus have coexisted for centuries, sharing festivals and shrines. In the nineteenth century, British observers wrote about Christians joining Hindu parades, carrying pictures of Saint Thomas alongside their neighbours' images of Hindu deities.

At the bookshop, a nun tried to sell me a Saint Thomas medallion. She had a tough look about her, the significance of which I didn't grasp until I left the shop and took a look at the shiny new mini-shrine outside it. It was a memorial to another bookshop worker, the shrine manager known only as Mr Jacob, who was stabbed and killed in the shop in November 2006 by a man who was variously described in reports I read later as a Hindu fanatic or mentally ill. The plaque on the memorial wasn't shy about drawing parallels: 'He was killed by a fanatic while defending the Christian ownership of this holy hill ... shedding blood in this very spot for his Lord and his God after the model of St Thomas, the apostle martyr of this shrine.'

If the martyred Saint Thomas was the most well known Christian figure in India, I could see how Graham Staines fitted so well into the country's Christian mythology.

The last stop on the Thomas trail was the San Thome Cathedral, by the beach in what seems like an upmarket neighbourhood. This is where Thomas is supposed to be buried. A series of churches have been built on the site, the current one an architecturally unexciting neo-Gothic structure with tall spires that was built in 1833. The basement tomb behind the cathedral is even less historically interesting. It was renovated in 2004 and evokes more than anything else the feel of a cheap conference centre, all pale faux-marble surfaces, tacky brasswork and blown-up pictures of Pope Benedict's visit. The centrepiece, above the door through to the centre of the tomb, is a huge reproduction of Caravaggio's painting *The Incredulity of St Thomas* (also known as *My Lord and My God*), showing Thomas poking his finger into the spear wound in Christ's side. A statue of Thomas's body lies over the spot where his actual remains are said to be. Dozens of people were kneeling in prayer around it when I was there.

Above ground, the small museum contains old tombstones, letters from popes and Thomas-related items of varying degrees of historic dubiousness. Part of the lance that killed the apostle is housed in a complicated reliquary topped with a cross. History and legend mix seamlessly in the attached plaques.

We drove back to the Y past Annie Besant Park, the Laughing Buddha Restaurant, Zion Church and hundreds more religious and commercial enterprises or combinations of the two, all crammed up against each other. A sign on the awning of a classy-looking sari shop read 'Designer clothes for the discerning woman', and just outside a filthy old woman wearing two knotted-together rags was tending a rubbish fire. It was the kind of juxtaposition that we developed-world writers in developing-world countries love to notice, because of course there are no inequalities, no very rich or very poor people, in our perfect home countries.

Posters and billboards all across the city were display-ing the current goddess of Tamil Nadu, Jayalalithaa, former chief minister of the state, now opposition leader and brilliant self-promoter. Jayalalithaa was previously a curvaceous film actress called Jayalalitha. She starred alongside MG Ramchandran, or MGR, the Tamil film legend turned much-loved chief minister of the state, and became his mistress. When MGR died, in 1987, she fought against his widow to gain control of his political party, added an extra 'a' to her name for numerological auspiciousness, and by most accounts brought a frightening new level of corruption, cronyism and self-serving bullshit to Tamil politics.

Most of the posters around Chennai were big colour portraits of Jayalalithaa, whose curves have become more and more pronounced over the years, and many of them contained a smaller, often sepia-toned image of MGR in a film role as Krishna or in his later oversized-sunglasses years, just to remind people of the connection. A few days earlier, a Tamil Chennai-based Hindu-turned-atheist-turned-Muslim musician called AR Rahman had become the temporary king of Chennai after he won two Academy Awards for the *Slumdog Millionaire* score. And a whole new batch of Jayalalithaa posters had gone up overnight, in which she had been Photoshopped standing next to Rahman, with a row of gold Oscars underneath them.

We were back at the Y by late afternoon. I hadn't spoken much to the driver, whose English was more limited than that of most south Indians I've met, but I wanted to know if the posters were working. 'Everywhere I'm seeing Jayalalithaa,' I said, as I climbed out of the car. 'What do you think, is she a good politician?'

He took my rupees and said, 'Jayalalithaa, she is mother to us all.' Then he smiled. 'Also, she is like you,' he added, sketching a wide hourglass in the air with his hands.

I waited in the lobby for a bearded American to finish his allotted half-hour at the communal computer. Across the room, a woman was bent over, sweeping the floor. She was thin, dark and weathered, with bad teeth and a threadbare rag of a sari. Another woman—coffee-coloured, glossy-haired, fat and wearing a silk sari—came out of the office and spoke with her in Tamil. They laughed together, clearly sharing a joke. It was a small scene, but it surprised me because it was such a genuine, equal interaction between two people who were so obviously of different castes and statuses. I remembered seeing a similar tableau played out in China a couple of years earlier and thinking 'You'd never see that in India.' I reminded myself that one untranslated conversation couldn't tell me anything real about the state of caste relations in modern India, but it was one of many tiny incidents that gave me a feeling that, in urban areas at least, the old certainties of class, caste and social status are slowly coming apart.

The lobby television had been switched over from temple television to local news. The main story was that the Chennai High Court was on fire after violent altercations between lawyers and police. I couldn't follow the complicated political background to the story. The cameras showed a barrister in his robes, hair askew, blood on his face and streaming bright-red down onto his white shirt, running out of a burning building. Behind him was fire.

That night I had a vivid and distressing series of dreams in which all the romantic breakups of my life were replayed. The next morning, while I was eating pooris and alu in the dining room at the Y, I tried to shake the images. I pop-diagnosed myself: It's about rejection. Hebron used to be my home, and now I'm not part of that world any more. It's a good thing too.

Across the room, I heard an Australian accent. A woman who looked about twenty years old was standing at the buffet table, asking about the pooris.

'Fried Indian bread, madam,' the waiter told her.

'I'll just have the boiled egg,' she said, smiling, and took a plate to her table.

I kept watching her. Unlike almost every young traveller I had ever seen in India, she looked clean and fresh. She wore a floral blouse, a white linen skirt and a face full of makeup. I had to know what she was doing there, so I took my plate of pooris to her table and said hello.

The young woman was also called Kate, and she was also from Melbourne; she giggled at the coincidence. She had flown in to Chennai twenty-four hours earlier, on her own, having never before left Australia. She was training to be a teacher and had arranged through an Indian friend to do a teaching round at an international school. I told her about my background, and she asked me questions about food and etiquette, and I held forth, lecturing her in the manner of someone who would call themselves an 'old India hand', which is a phrase I would never use.

'I like your suit,' she said.

I advised her to invest in a salwar kameez for herself—they're cool and comfortable and modest, I said, and much easier to wear than a sari.

'Am I dressed okay?' she asked.

I patronised her, saying, 'You might find white isn't very practical: it'll get grubby.'

She nodded, deferring to me.

I wondered how many minutes her makeup would last in the heat of Chennai. I never wear makeup in India unless I'm in the cool hills; it mixes with sweat and slides straight off my face.

I wished her good luck and, with the glow that comes with having imparted wisdom, I went about my day.

That evening, back in the dining room, while I was scoffing saag paneer, Kate waved at me from across the room and carried her plate over. Her makeup was still perfect, and her skirt was still spotless. I asked about her day, expecting to hear about culture shock, about dirt and beggars and inability to communicate, at which point I would tell her that even after all these years I felt that way on my first days back, that it was understandable.

'I had a fantastic time,' she said.

She had walked around the streets near the Y, and everyone she had met had been friendly and kind. Chancing upon a building that looked like a school, she had wandered in, because she was interested in education in India, and someone had taken her to meet the principal, who turned out to be a woman and had shown her around the school, which turned out to be a girls college, and had introduced her to the students, and they had told her about their lives, and they had admired each other's clothes.

'So what did you do today?' she asked.

I sighed, realising that I was not nearly as good a traveller as Kate was.

My original plan for the day had been to visit a Sufi shrine. I had been reading about Sufism in India, about how it often seems to combine Muslim and Hindu traditions. I had wanted to discover tolerance and syncretism in the Indian religious tradition; I had wanted to know that what happened to Graham Staines was an exception.

Sufism is generally more widespread in north India than in the south, but I had found an online reference to a shrine in the silk-producing temple town of Kanchipuram, a couple of hours away from Chennai by bus. Hamid Shah Awliya was apparently a Tamil Sufi saint whose shrine has become the focus of Hindu pilgrimage and devotion over the last few centuries.

I had visited a Muslim shrine to a saint called Natther years before, in the southern Tamil town of Trichy; I had carefully covered my head with my dupatta, the scarf of my salwar kameez, and hoped my presence wouldn't cause offence. In fact, a group of men who spoke no English had welcomed me with friendly gestures, walked me to the carved door of the inner shrine and showed me how to press my hands together in worship in a way that looked traditionally Hindu to me. Unexpectedly, one of the men had then touched my head and shoulders with a bundle of peacock feathers and given me a handful of almonds to eat. I had no idea what this meant. The men had all smiled and waved as I departed.

But on my second morning in Chennai, going on a long excursion to an unknown town had just felt too hard. Perhaps the culture shock I'd expected to see in Kate was a projection of my own feelings of dread about hot weather and long, crowded bus trips and having to ask directions from strangers who would no doubt all send me in different directions. I had also fully expected to come down with Saint Thomas miracle spring lurgy, which would have been hellish on a local bus. I had told Kate that I'm a Lonely Planet author, which now made my ineptitude even more embarrassing.

Instead of having an adventure in Kanchipuram, I had caught an autorickshaw to the government museum, which had proved to be an adventure of sorts when the driver had first taken me to a souvenir emporium that he insisted was the museum. When I had insisted that it wasn't, he said the museum was shut today, which was why he had kindly taken me here instead. I had shouted at him, and he had driven me to the museum.

Images of deities are everywhere in India. You see shrines to Kali on the streets, tiny statues of Ganesh placed above doorways in homes, house-sized Krishnas outside temples, paintings of Lakshmi on autorickshaws, images of Hanuman on the backs of trucks, Devi stickers attached to paan sellers' carts. Spend any time in India and the various members of the pantheon become like familiar old friends. The artistic quality of the images varies wildly; most of the statues and paintings are cheaply mass-produced, or homemade by amateurs or folk artists.

Only occasionally, at museums like Chennai's, have I seen such beautiful, perfectly proportioned work of real craftspeople. They had been dead for centuries, of course. But the bronzes, in particular, were lovely. I stood in front of a rendering of Nataraj, Shiva dancing in a circle of stylised flames. There was the fire, again. A plaque explained that the image had a scientific meaning, that it represented atoms flying around a nucleus. I doubted this was a traditional interpretation, but I liked it.

The role of fire in Hindu ritual and imagery seems to fascinate outsiders. Its symbolism as cleanser and destroyer—the image of the holy fire lit in temples that is central to weddings and other ceremonies—is something I dwelled on a lot in regard to the death of Graham Staines. I wondered for a while whether this was why his murder had provoked such a strong reaction across India: it seemed to me that the nature of his death struck people as particularly horrific—as opposed to if he had been, say, beaten up or shot.

But of course you don't have to be Hindu, or Indian, to feel that way, and I'm wary of making claims about how Graham's death by fire was somehow significant to Indian people because of the role of fire in their cultural tradition: I'm not qualified to make that kind of interpretation. I might have grown up in India, but I have to accept that the way I saw the country at the time I lived there—its culture, history and people— was filtered both through missionaries and through foreign writers and filmmakers, who made for some pretty suspect sources. It's why I don't want to see *Slumdog Millionaire*, an Indian story told by a British screenwriter and director.

After all, my knowledge that fire is important in Hinduism came mainly from watching *The Jewel in the Crown*, the 1984 miniseries based on Paul Scott's Raj Quartet novels and set among the British in India in the 1940s. Hebron School's limited video library contained a copy of the series, and one term when I was about fourteen the kids in my year watched all the episodes over seven Saturday nights. Scott developed the theme of fire in the books, and it was also central to the television series. The resulting images stayed with me for years.

In an early episode an elderly missionary called Edwina Crane is beaten and her Indian colleague is killed by a crowd inflamed with anti-British sentiment. Miss Crane recovers in hospital but then returns home and commits suicide, dressing herself in white and setting herself aflame in imitation of an Indian widow on her husband's funeral pyre.

Later in the series a young English woman, Susan Bingham, hears about Miss Crane's death. She becomes unbalanced after her husband dies, leaving her with a young baby. She puts her baby down on the lawn and makes a circle of fire around him using kerosene and matches. Mesmerised by the flames, she hardly notices when the Indian nurse rushes in to save the baby. The music and camera work make it clear that there is something mystical and exotic about fire in Indian culture, and that it is affecting the British. At the time I adored the series; it was intense and sad and sexy and full of meaning, I thought.

It was awful, awful stuff to be showing white adolescents living in India in the 1980s. I didn't think at the time about how my Indian school friends must have felt, watching this story that exoticised their culture while at the same time sidelining the Indian characters. Salman Rushdie's criticism of the books and series hit me hard when I read his essay 'Outside the Whale': 'The Quartet's form tells us, in effect, that the history of the end of the Raj was largely composed of the doings of the officer class and its wife. Indians get walk-ons, but remain, for the most part, bit-players in their own history.'

We never watched Indian-made films, but we watched those by the British about India: *The Far Pavilions*, with Amy Irving and Christopher Lee in blackface, Richard Attenborough's *Gandhi*, with Ben Kingsley in blackface, and *A Passage to India*, with Alec Guinness in blackface.

I had never considered buying a statue of a Hindu deity before. When I was a Christian, I would have thought it wrong to support the manufacture of idols, and offensive to Indian Christians for me to display such a thing. I might have worried that it would bring an evil spirit into my house. By the time I was no longer a Christian, I would have thought of it as cultural appropriation—putting an Indian deity on my shelf would make me look like a stupid white hippy. But the images at the Chennai Museum were so appealing that I began to reason with myself that it was perfectly acceptable for me, as a chubby writer, to own an image of Ganesh, the elephant god, holding his broken tusk in his hand; one story relates that he broke it off and used it to write the Mahabharata.

At about midday I realised it had been twenty-four hours since I drank the miracle water and I was not sick. ('That's the miracle,' Chris said that evening, when I phoned him from the Y.)

I sat down on a bench opposite some carved memorial stones. I thought at first they must be Muslim, because they all contained an image of a crescent moon. But the moon had a different meaning here: these were sati stones, memorials for women who had been burned alive on their husband's funeral pyre. They showed the woman, or sometimes just her arms, wearing bangles, which indicated that she was a wife, not a widow. On each stone there was an image of the husband looking down at his wife, and of the sun and moon, which indicated that her name would be remembered as long as the sun and moon exist. Which, of course, is wrong. Her death by fire made her a symbol of piety to be memorialised, but names get forgotten. Five years earlier, everyone had wanted to talk about Graham Staines and his sacrifice, but memories are short. I thought about the educated young honeymooners on the hill train who said they'd never heard of him.

The next day I caught an early-morning bus south of Chennai to Mamallapuram, a beachside temple town. When my family first moved to India, our holidays were spent travelling to obscure destinations to visit different kinds of missionaries. We went to hospitals and agriculture projects and Adivasi, or tribal, villages in hard-to-reach places. But after the first year or two, we began to gravitate towards beach towns like Mamallapuram, Kovalam and Goa, where we could swim in the ocean and eat fresh fish curries and banana pancakes. These were the only places in India, outside Ooty, in which I ever talked to other foreigners.

Once, in Goa, when I was about nine years old, we became friendly with an American family staying in the same hotel as us. They were doing some sort of Christian work in Mumbai and had a daughter about my age, and we swam and played on the beach together. One day, on a Saturday, I couldn't find my friend, and I asked my mother where she might be. My mother explained that the family were Seventh-Day Adventists, and Saturday was their Sabbath, so she couldn't come outside and play. I don't think I had ever heard of Seventh-Day Adventists, and from the way my mother described them it was not at all clear to me whether they were saved or not. If they weren't saved, I thought, if they weren't real Christians, then what a terrible waste for them to be here in India, doing good works and trying to help people, but being wrong themselves.

As I have continued to travel to India as an adult, I have found that beach towns are still the best place to meet other foreigners. And as I have spoken to them in thatched-hut restaurants over Kingfisher beers and banana pancakes, I have formed the opinion that there are two main—and distinct—types of travellers in India.

The first type—more often male, but not always— is a seasoned traveller who is happy to admit they are in India just to enjoy themselves. They make no apologies for being in a tourist town. They like the food, and sometimes the cheap drugs, and they talk loudly and cheerfully to Indian waiters and rickshaw drivers, calling them 'buddy' or 'mate'. They're often on their way to or from Thailand or Sri Lanka. One such traveller, a bleach-blond Scandinavian, once described himself to me as a 'crazy pahdy ahnimal'. He knocked on my door in the middle of the night, drunk, and then apologised the next day. 'I only do this because you made me horny,' he explained.

The other kind of traveller is usually just as patronising and ignorant when it comes to any real knowledge about India and its people, but hides it better. These are the hippies, the seekers, the travellers who claim to be drawn to the country because of its beautiful spirituality. They are often slightly embarrassed to be caught in a banana pancake town. In Mamallapuram they claim to be just passing through on their way to Tiruvannamallai, where they will join the Hindu pilgrims walking around Annamalai Hill and up to the fire temple. 'This place is too touristy; Tiru is where it's at now,' they say.

Frankly, I like the crazy pahdy ahnimals slightly better than the hippies. I'm not nuts about any of them. And I keep going back to spend more time with them.

The bus pulled up outside the Talasayana Perumai Temple in the centre of Mamallapuram, and I ducked down a side street, away from the rickshaw drivers. A little girl, maybe about eight years old, followed me. She was wearing a dirty cotton dress and had strings of beads draped over her arm. She waved the beads at me, calling 'Madam, madam.'

'*Vendam*,' I said, using a useful Tamil word that means 'Don't want'.

The girl laughed and kept following me, rattling the beads. 'You buy, madam,' she said, over and over.

'No,' I said, continuing to walk.

The girl changed tack. Instead of laughing, she started to whine, touching her hand to her mouth. 'No food, madam, no food,' she said. 'You give me money.'

I kept walking.

'Rupees, give me rupees,' she said.

The girl came right up to me and tugged at my arm.

I pulled away quickly and without thinking I hissed at her, the same '*Tss*' sound I use when my dogs misbehave. For a moment, I was furious that she had touched me.

The girl laughed again and skipped away.

I felt sick. I hated myself.

People sometimes assume that because I've spent a lot of time in India, because I have written about it for Lonely Planet, I know how to behave in such situations. But I don't have any answers. When I behave like that, it makes me wonder whether I have any right to be in India at all.

I kept walking, making my way from memory towards Arjuna's Penance, a series of bas relief carvings in the sandy rocks that are possibly the most gorgeous, naturalistic pieces of ancient art I've ever seen. My main memories of the scenes were that they include an army of almost life-sized elephants and that the titular Arjuna is a very thin sage who stands on one leg. I'd forgotten all the little details like the baby elephants huddled under their mother, and the cat standing in the same meditative pose as Arjuna, in front of a group of mice. Alongside the sage and the elephants are carved nagas, snake people, looking almost identical to the carved mermaid on the altar at St Thomas Mount. Only the headwear is different—the snake people have cobra-like hoods instead of Christian crosses on their heads.

Alongside me, Indian visitors photographed the carvings. Just up the road, a group of European tourists were taking pictures of the Krishna Mandapam, a temple cut out of the same piece of rock as Arjuna's Penance. I walked towards them and realised they were photographing only the roof of the temple. A couple of goats had wandered over the rocks and were now sitting up there, chewing on some overhanging branches. For some reason the foreigners thought this a wonderful picture opportunity.

A little Indian girl wearing a satin salwar kameez pulled on her father's sleeve. 'Why they are shooting the goats, Daddy?' she asked. He shooshed her, but it was a fair enough question. Goats are everywhere in India. Perhaps the Europeans thought a goat on a temple roof made a more charming scene than a goat in a pile of rubbish.

I walked down to the beach and along by the water and then cut up Othavadai Street, which is lined with banana pancake restaurants, Kashmiri souvenir shops and tailors selling baggy cotton clothes that most Indian people wouldn't dream of wearing. A board outside a shop advertised Ayurvedic massages 'recommended by Lonely Planet'. Which, to be fair, they are.

I hadn't been in India long enough to be craving pancakes or conversation with hippies. I actually wanted to go back to Chennai and eat curry and pickles at the Y. An air-conditioned bus was just pulling away when I reached the stop outside the temple; I waved at the driver and he slowed down—without entirely stopping—so that I could swing up the steps.

We drove along the highway. Ten years earlier, when I travelled south on the coastal road, the view from the bus window had been of thatched huts, palm trees and rice paddies. But now the highway outside Chennai is lined with what look like spaceships: huge, gleaming chrome-and-glass buildings with names like Cybercorp, Infotech and Technisource; they sound like Homer Simpson's internet start-up, Compuglobalhypermeganet.

The elderly man sitting across from me was staring at the buildings with what seemed to me to be deep sadness and confusion, but I had to remind myself that I couldn't know what he was thinking. The buildings might not be pretty, but they had brought jobs to Chennai. Sometimes, changes just take some getting used to.

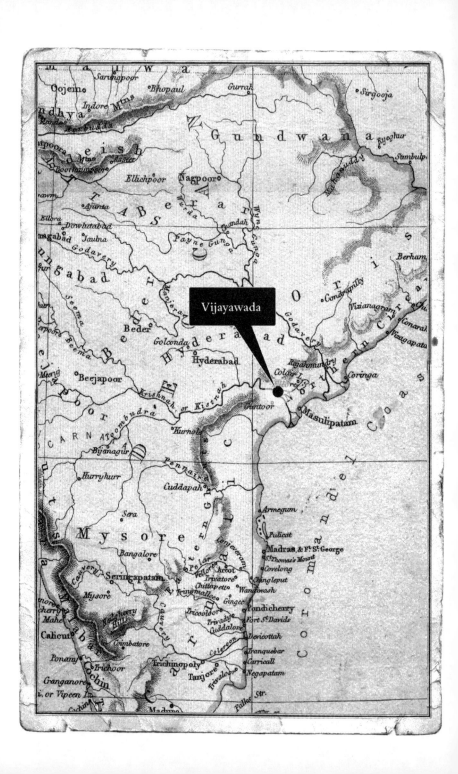

3

VIJAYAWADA

It was my father who led me to the atheists of Vijayawada, the next stop on my trip. He bought Richard Dawkins's *The God Delusion*, a book that I wouldn't have thought to spend money on myself, but when I saw it on my parents' bookshelf I asked if I could borrow it, along with Christopher Hitchens's *God Is Not Great*, and I read them both over a long weekend, lying on a banana lounge in the backyard with the dogs sleeping across my feet. I loosely agreed with a lot of what both writers said, but neither book made a huge impact on me other than to remind me that Christopher Hitchens can be a bit of a dick. I had rejected Christianity for myself nearly ten years earlier.

I don't think the kinds of arguments rehashed by Dawkins and Hitchens were what pushed me away from Christianity, or if they were I hadn't consciously realised it. When I was still a Christian, or trying to be a Christian, I saw any argument against my faith as an opportunity to come up with an even better riposte. But looking back now, I wouldn't be surprised if some of those arguments—all the old classics like Bertrand Russell's teapot, why a good and omnipotent deity would allow suffering, what would happen in the afterlife to those who had never heard of Christianity, and so on—perniciously ate away at my faith like termites in foundations, eventually helping to bring down my whole house.

In any case, in the back pages of *The God Delusion* Dawkins lists atheist and humanist organisations around the world, including a couple in India. I got online to follow the links and surfed a wave of Indian humanism until I washed up among the atheists of Vijayawada.

Goparaju Ramachandra Rao, known as Gora, was a twentieth-century Indian atheist, a friend of Mahatma Gandhi, and a contemporary of Vinayak Damodar Savarkar, the founder of the Hindutva. Born a high-caste Brahmin in Orissa in 1902, Gora was an orthodox young man who studied botany and became a college lecturer. In his early twenties, not long after he married a ten-year-old girl called Saraswathi, he was offered work at an American college on the condition that he convert to Christianity. He refused, but the idea started him thinking about religion. He read a lot, spent some time living with Buddhist monks in Sri Lanka and talked to his young wife. In 1928, when Saraswathi was sixteen, the couple declared themselves atheists.

In the following years Gora wrote a lot of books exploring all kinds of political, psychological and philosophical aspects of atheism, but it all came down to this, written in his short book *We Become Atheists*: 'It appeared to me that people closed their minds with faith in god and fate. They lost initiative, became superstitious and fanatically clung to their beliefs. But god and fate were beliefs with no basis in reality. They were falsehoods. If we reject them, we stand on our feet, feel free, work well, and live equal, since all of us belong to the same kind.'

In 1940, after being dismissed from various lecturing positions because of his publicly declared atheism (which, in India, translated pretty much as 'wickedness'), Gora moved his family to a thatched hut in a village called Mudunur in Andhra Pradesh and divided his time between working for the Quit India movement against the British, where he met Gandhi, and establishing the Atheist Centre. The centre ran activities ranging from science education to organising inter-caste meals and marriages. Locals liked and supported the family, and Mudunur became known as 'the godless village'. Saraswathi took her irreligiousness one step further by permanently taking off her jewellery, as bangles and necklaces have religious significance in traditional

Hindu culture. Soon after the move she was sent to jail for six months for protesting against British rule.

Nine children were born to Gora and Saraswathi, and they all married outside their caste. When their daughter Manorama married a dalit, untouchable, called Arjun Rao in 1960, it was still an unthinkable idea to most people, and it made the national newspapers.

Just before Independence, in 1947, the Atheist Centre shifted to a suburb of Vijayawada, the second-biggest city in Andhra Pradesh. It's still there. Gora died in 1975 and Saraswathi in 2006. The centre is run mainly by their surviving children and grandchildren, who share the work with atheists, Christians, Muslims and Hindus who work at the attached hospital, women's refuge and street-kid shelter. Science education and inter-caste meetings are still on the agenda, along with disaster relief. Teams travel to villages and run 'magic camps' for children in which they demonstrate how the miracles performed by 'godmen' are simple tricks. They say their goal is to plant the seeds of scepticism.

A few weeks before I left Australia I had emailed the centre and heard back almost immediately from one of the elder Gora sons, Dr Vijayam, who encouraged me to visit and stay with them. By contrast, at around the same time I contacted a Melbourne-based evangelical mission that supported Indian Christian workers in Orissa. I knew they had been involved with helping the displaced and poor Christians whose homes had been torched during the recent communal conflict in the tribal areas of Orissa, and I hoped they could give me some contacts. But my many phone calls and emails to the mission went unanswered.

A number of times, in the course of my evangelical childhood, I read books and heard sermons that asked me to consider, as proof of the truth and goodness of religion, and particularly of Christianity, that there was no such thing as an atheist-run orphanage. I still don't know if such a thing exists, but through my stay at the Atheist Centre, I did manage to visit an atheist-run hospital, an atheist-run shelter for street children and an atheist-run refuge for victims of domestic abuse.

I travelled to Vijayawada in an air-conditioned compartment after getting up at four o'clock to catch the daytime train from Chennai. I watched rural Andhra Pradesh go past, all fields and broad, shallow rivers and rice paddies, while I listened to a book on my iPod—Barack Obama reading his autobiography, *Dreams from My Father*. I knew all about political realities, but the idea that such a thoughtful man, with such broad experience of other cultures, had become the president of the United States still felt like—for want of a better word—some kind of miracle.

When I arrived in Vijayawada I caught an auto-rickshaw to the Atheist Centre, a collection of old buildings around a courtyard, one side of which is attached to a big, new-looking hospital. The auto driver didn't recognise 'Nasthik Kendram', the Telugu name for the centre, but he knew 'Dr Samaram hospital'. Dr Samaram is perhaps the most well known of Gora's children; in addition to managing the hospital, he writes a syndicated sex-advice column and has published a series of books about sexual health. In 2010 he was named head of the Indian Medical Association.

I was greeted by Dr Vijayam, who took me into the family home to meet a few of his various siblings, children, nephews and nieces who happened to be about. I repeated their names but, in most cases, promptly forgot them. Vijayam's sister, Mithri, told me that instead of giving their children the names of gods or goddesses, which is the norm in India, Gora and Saraswathi had named them after events, ideas and ideologies. Vijayam means 'victory'. This idea had been carried into the next generation: among Gora's grandchildren were Demos ('democracy'), Suez (born in the year the canal was opened) and Haley (after the comet).

I drank tea at the big dining table with Mithri and Vijayam, under an oil painting of Saraswathi, while some of the other women busied themselves in the kitchen. There were seventy-three descendants of Gora currently alive, Mithri said, and they all identified as atheists. Vijayam added that there was no pressure on them to do this, that they were not 'born atheist'.

I very much wanted this to be true, and I thought about my grandmother. In the past she spoke at every family gathering about her thankfulness that all her children and grandchildren had chosen to follow the Lord, but she doesn't say this any more, presumably because of me. She sincerely believes that each other member of the family recognised their need for the Lord of their own free will, and I'm sure they would all tell you this is true. Nobody is 'born Christian', my grandmother would say. But whereas I would once have said that I made my own informed decision to be a Christian too, now I don't think I really did. I don't believe it's possible for a five-year-old to make a genuinely considered choice when her loving parent asks hopefully if she'd like to say a prayer to ask Jesus into her heart. And the eager-to-please teenager who doesn't know anyone who isn't a Christian isn't in a much better position.

Some of the Goras work at the centre, while others are scattered around India. There are a lot of doctors among them. One of the Gora grandchildren, a sweet-faced and friendly young woman called Supa, wandered in and was introduced. She is a singer, I was told, who recently returned from studying philosophy in Canada. She was followed in by her cousin Demos, a paediatrician, who was on her way to work and had dropped by to hand her baby son over to Vijayam; he happily bounced him on his knee. After she left, Mithri told me that Demos is an accomplished classical dancer who has performed traditional religious dances to much acclaim, but that she also dances at atheist events in schools and villages, telling dance-stories about AIDS prevention and the theory of evolution.

It took me a while to work out what was different about the women of the Atheist Centre. Eventually I realised that, like Saraswathi, none of them wear jewellery. 'My father said, "For my daughters, their education is their ornament,"' Mithri told me.

The whole extended family set-up with the shared kitchen, dining area and babysitting duties is typically Indian, but in other ways the family is clearly different. Unlike most professionals they have no servants; instead, they share the menial jobs between them. They are welcoming hosts, but they don't fawn; perhaps you need to have travelled as a Westerner in India to realise how unusual this is. When I copied Supa's example and washed my own teacup at the sink, nobody rushed to stop me. Nobody called me 'madam', which was a welcome change; they called me Kate.

After Vijayam had asked a few polite questions about my family and then told me a lot about the centre, more family members appeared, and a simple lunch of rice and dahl was served up. I was introduced to Niyanta, a younger and more energetic version of Vijayam, who seemed to have been given the job of ferrying me around with him for the next few days. 'Tonight we're all going to a wedding, so you can come too,' he said. He assured me that there would be hundreds, maybe thousands, of guests, and there would be no problem with me joining them.

I went to take a rest in my room, which was basic and cluttered. The floor was made of worn paving stones, there were a couple of battered plastic chairs, and pages from out-of-date calendars and random colourful posters (cats, and an enormously fat baby with huge, moist eyes) were taped to the walls. The adjoining exposed-concrete bathroom had a flush toilet but no shower, which was more than I had expected. A pile of books and pamphlets by and about Gora sat next to the bed. There was a two-storey-high mango tree just outside the door; at lunch I had been warned that a mango might fall on my head. One of the women had made a joke about my hair being the colour of a mango already.

I had a bucket bath and lay down, but I didn't sleep. I did some yogic breathing and enjoyed being alone and not straining for conversation. I liked the Goras. In many ways it was a relief to be among people who agreed when I told the truth about what I believe, or don't believe. I knew that when I reached the mission in Baripada I would be among Christians and would have to strain the truth about myself or be disapproved of; there would probably be a bit of both. But the Goras' accents were strong and I was tired, and for everything we had in common there were cultural differences that

I couldn't always anticipate; I was tense with trying to understand and not wanting to offend.

I hardly had a wedding wardrobe with me, but when it was time to get ready for the evening ahead I put on my brightest kameez, in apple green with an orange-gold border that matched my hair, and hoped it would suffice. The Gora women all wore beautiful silk saris, without the jewellery that usually accompanies wedding clothes.

The actual wedding had already taken place at the Hindu temple. We arrived for the reception, a massive affair held in the biggest hall of the local college. On the way, as the sun was setting, Niyanta told me that he and his brothers had made national headlines in the 1960s by protesting over this college's application form, which had mandatory 'religion' and 'caste' categories and would not accept 'none' as answers. The Goras had written to India's education minister to object. 'The matter was discussed even in the state legislative assembly,' Niyanta said. It was eventually decided that, because India is a secular state, the Goras had a genuine case. 'The question was made optional in the college form and our answer "none" to caste and religion was accepted.' But the questions are still included on the form, even now.

Outside, the hall was covered in fairy lights that flashed in elaborate patterns. Other lights spelled out the names of the bride and groom. Inside, a brass band was playing, and hundreds of people milled around under fluorescent tube lights. We joined a queue to greet the couple, who were seated on the stage under a canopy. Little girls wearing glittery dresses held baskets of marigold petals for us to sprinkle on them.

I put my hands together and said 'Namaste' to them, and they returned the greeting, not registering any surprise that a mango-headed foreigner they'd never met was chucking petals at them. They both had layers of flowers draped around their necks already, and their eyes looked glazed; I imagined it had been a long day for them, though it was far from over.

We moved on to the main event: stuffing yourself at someone else's expense. Buffet tables outside were covered in masses of food. I was disappointed that I'd filled up on rice and dahl in the afternoon—I was too full and tired to take advantage of the spread and instead just gaped at the haze of stunning, bright-coloured saris and brilliant jewellery. Yet for all the glitzy outfits, I thought the most beautiful woman there was Dr Demos, jewel-free in her pink sari. Her face was lovely, and there was no doubt that part of her loveliness was her intelligence. Demos stayed close to me, and I felt as if she was looking after me. I really, really wished I could see her dance about the theory of evolution.

I fell asleep briefly in the car on the way back to the centre. After we had arrived and drunk more tea, Vijayam told me that I would be speaking at a public meeting the next morning for Science Day. 'The theme is astronomy,' he said.

I felt suddenly sick. I told Vijayam that I'm not much of a speaker, but it appeared that there was no way out.

'The media will be there,' he added, as an afterthought.

This was not something I had expected, though perhaps I should have. In the past I'd been asked to preach at short notice when visiting Indian Christians. Maybe it is presumed that all Westerners are articulate and have wisdom to impart, or perhaps they just think it's polite to ask. A few years earlier, when I was in Kerala, I had visited a Salvation Army project to deliver a gift from my parents to a little girl they sponsored in a poor community. What I didn't realise was that the whole community was going to gather to hang garlands around my neck and hear me preach. I had already come out of the closet as a nonbeliever at home, but I just didn't have it in me to do it among Indian Christians, and I threw together a trite little talk that I would rather die than ever repeat to anyone.

This time I decided I'd just have to cheat. I set my alarm for early and went straight to sleep, and in the morning I had another bucket bath then got out my iPod and searched through my audio books until I found a passage from Bill Bryson's *A Short History of Nearly Everything*, a vaguely diverting story about an Australian amateur astronomer. I took some notes and simplified the message, such as it was (astronomy is kind of cool and interesting) and ended up with an innocuous talk with reference to my own country in which I didn't have to lie—a better result than I might have hoped for.

After I had eaten piles of breakfast idlis with the family, Vijayam led me to a hall in which rows of plastic chairs had been set up. Outside, posters in English and Telugu told the stories of Galileo and Copernicus. A couple of photographers asked me to pose in front of the posters. Then I sat on the stage with the other speakers—Vijayam, Niyanta and a real live physicist— before a half-full hall of what I was told were students and teachers, and supporters of the centre.

The other talks were given in Telugu. Niyanta included some YouTube clips projected onto a screen about the life of Galileo. After he introduced me, Niyanta said he would translate for me. My little talk was followed by polite applause. Niyanta had obviously given it his own slant, as I'd recognised 'Bible', 'Einstein', 'seeing is believing' and 'Hubble Telescope' in his translation, none of which was in my version. I didn't mind. The Gora brothers are practised public speakers, and everyone listened to them intently. I'm sure my talk was improved.

Afterwards, I was collared by a pushy old bore in a gleaming-white kurta who gave me his life story. Raised by peasants, he had become proprietor of the Popular

Shoe Mart despite his not going on pilgrimages or doing things at astrologically auspicious times or consulting priests or giving money to temples. I could read all about it in this publication, he told me, handing me a booklet called *Beliefs & Truths*. 'My experiences and my thoughts should not be limited to me, my family and workers in our establishments only,' he declared on the back cover.

Niyanta eventually rescued me, greeting the important man deferentially while steering me away from him. Then he told me that after lunch we would visit a school, where I would talk to the children about 'science and the scientific method'. I wanted to tell him that I was terrible at science at school, and that I'm scared to death of public speaking, and that this wasn't what I'd signed up for. But again, I didn't feel I had much of a choice. I decided to recycle the morning's talk—what could he do, give me poor marks for not staying on topic?

The school was a nominally Hindu set-up for boys from lower castes, though the word 'caste' was never used. When Niyanta and I arrived we were taken to meet the principal, who described the boys to me as 'poor children', 'some even the children of sweepers'. He shouted at a peon to bring us tea and biscuits. Various deities were displayed in brightly coloured posters on the office wall, and a large blue ceramic Krishna sat in the corner. It was a bit dusty.

After Niyanta and I had been paraded through the first of many classrooms, I realised we were looking at a science fair, a collection of science-related projects on topics the boys had chosen for themselves. The students stood next to their exhibits and explained how they worked and what they showed. They had done a great job, especially considering how limited their resources must have been. There were motorised toy boats, dioramas, hydroponic plants, clay models of the evolution of man next to a picture of Darwin, a styrofoam man with a battery-operated bionic arm, and that old classic—the erupting volcano. I nodded and smiled and said 'Very good' at each explanation. The boys smiled back and looked pleased with themselves. They all wore white shirts and khaki shorts, though some of the uniforms looked pretty faded.

When the tour was over, Niyanta and I sat on a stage with the teachers, outside in the schoolyard. The boys sat on the dusty ground with their legs crossed. I did my talk again, adding a few comments about how what we learn in science class has wider ramifications. I said that if we learn to look for evidence and search for the truth for ourselves, we won't be exploited by politicians or advertisers (or priests, I didn't say). Niyanta gave another suspect translation and then delivered his own talk about the importance of science, which was transfixing even in Telugu, and the boys listened carefully.

I was then asked to present prizes for the best exhibits. Names were read out, boys paraded across the stage, and I handed them a calico bag or a plastic bowl and shook their hand while somebody took a photo. When all the prizes were gone, a teacher presented Niyanta with a small clock and gave me a book inscribed 'To Kits, Australia', and then we all sang the Indian national anthem, 'Jana Gana Mana', and school was out for the day.

The book presented to me was French mystic Romain Rolland's *Life of Vivekananda*, a breathless biography of India's wandering Hindu monk and social reformer. I wouldn't have recognised many swamis, but I knew a little about Vivekananda. In the late nineteenth century he spoke at the Parliament of Religions in Chicago, bringing an attractive and likeable form of Hinduism to Western intellectuals, free-thinkers and spiritualists, who flocked to him and followed him around for the rest of his fairly short life. It was hard to blame them, after reading the address that brought him international attention. In it he said that Hinduism was a religion of toleration that accepted all religions as true and had sheltered Jews and Zoroastrians who had fled other countries. He quoted from a Vedic hymn: 'As the different streams having their sources in different paths which men take through different tendencies, various though they appear, crooked or straight, all lead to Thee.' He also said:

....

Sectarianism, bigotry, and its horrible descendant, fanaticism, have long possessed this beautiful earth. They have filled the earth with violence, drenched it often and often with human blood, destroyed civilization and sent whole nations to despair. Had it not been for these horrible demons, human society would be far more advanced than it is now. But their time is come; and I fervently hope that the bell that tolled this morning in honor of this convention may be the death-knell of all fanaticism, of all persecutions with the sword or with the pen, and of all uncharitable feelings between persons wending their way to the same goal.

....

Another reason I recognised Vivekananda was because he was very good-looking, of the slightly plump-faced, pillow-lipped, dark-eyed young-Elvis type that I particularly admire. I looked at him on the cover of the book in my room that night and was reminded of Parijat and Vivek and a few other Indian men I had known and fancied. These were not appropriate thoughts, I know.

During my talk, I had noticed that I was speaking with a strong Indian accent. It had been slowly creeping back ever since I landed in Coimbatore, though I wasn't doing it on purpose. My father used to do the same thing when he preached in India, speaking in Indian-English dialect because he assumed it made him easier for the translator to understand. Once, when we first returned to Australia from India, he was asked to preach with a translator at a Hungarian church, and he delivered the whole sermon in a broad Indian accent out of sheer force of habit. My mother tried to catch his eye from the pew, but even when you've been married for seventeen years it's hard to communicate 'You sound ridiculous' solely with eyebrow movements.

Back at the Goras' communal dining table I told Mithri that I was slipping into my Indian accent, and the singer-philosopher Supa smiled and said, 'Mithri told me before, "I can understand this lady so much more easily than other foreigners."' Mithri smiled in acknowledgement.

The next morning Niyanta took me to his Rotary meeting, a breakfast buffet get-together held in the conference room of an upmarket hotel. It was just a social occasion, he said; there wouldn't be any speeches. I noticed that only men attended and asked if there were any female Rotarians. Niyanta assured me there were, but he said they didn't tend to come to meetings. He introduced me to a few men, one of whom was an English teacher who was excited to hear that I work as an editor and interrogated me about style guides. Did I use *Strunk and White*? What did I think about *Chicago*? At each introduction, Niyanta, who knew very well what I was doing in India, said that I was 'on a study tour on the topic of people and their attitudes'.

I wasn't sure why he didn't want to mention Graham Staines; I wondered whether the topic was in some way embarrassing. I didn't know how to ask him about this, so I never discovered the reason he spoke this way.

We took the long way home via a river that fed into the sea, where a series of canals and locks had been built to help farmers irrigate their fields. We walked on a road running alongside the river while Niyanta described how the canals worked, and he used the subject as a jumping-off point to speak about the importance of science and practical work in helping to improve lives. Religion holds people back, he said. He spoke in generalities and platitudes that I agreed with, but I couldn't help feeling that he was in the habit of delivering lectures like this. We walked past a hand-painted sign with Telugu text that showed a middle-aged modern-looking man and woman kneeling before a young orange-clad monk, who was praying. The perspective was out of whack: the monk was much bigger than the couple.

'What does that say?' I asked.

'It's just something like "Pray to the Buddha,"' Niyanta replied. Vijayawada is actually something of a centre for Buddhism in south India, he told me.

We crossed a bridge with carvings on the suspension pillars showing the Buddha sitting under the Bodhi tree surrounded by bodhisattvas.

'The Buddha spoke some good philosophy, but people turned it into a religion,' Niyanta said.

I said I'd read about dalits, people of the untouchable class, who reject Hinduism and turn to Buddhism as a way to escape the caste system, and Niyanta agreed that this happens but said that ideally people should be without religion altogether, that all superstition holds people back.

The heat (and probably the pollution) created an attractively hazy effect on the view over the river towards the city. Green hills were visible in the distance, and fishing boats bobbed on the water. Niyanta said he would take me back to the centre, give me a tour of the hospital and show me how the Atheist Centre was fighting superstition.

The hospital was simple, clean and quiet. Books about AIDS by Dr Samaram filled the shelf in the waiting room. The walls in the entrance area were covered with big colour pictures with Telugu captions, showing how various religious miracles were actually performed. As a child I saw wandering sadhus with big metal spikes through their tongues—a picture here showed that the spike had a curve in it so it slipped over the tongue like a comedy arrow through the head. A statue of Ganesh that appeared to be drinking milk from a spoon had recently made the news, and another picture showed that the same effect could be achieved by feeding milk to a bottle of Mango Slice drink.

We dropped in to one of the offices to see Dr Samaram's wife, Rashmi, a smart and serious woman who manages the women's refuge and hostel. She was keen to tell me about all the organisations that had helped to fund their programs, including the Clinton Foundation. Behind her was a framed photo of her shaking hands with Bill Clinton. He looked so radiantly goddamn charming, focusing all his attention on her while she simpered like a schoolgirl.

Afterwards, Vijayam and his wife, Sumithi, were waiting for me, armed with a copy of the local paper in Telugu that had a photo of me and the other speakers at the previous day's science lecture. I walked with them to lunch at the house of a family who lived down the road. Like most of the Goras' friends they were Hindus, and their son was a school friend of one of Niyanta's sons. He had been sent to the United States to study and was now a software engineer. He and his wife were visiting his parents to show off their first child, a baby son, and the whole neighbourhood had been invited to lunch to celebrate the new arrival.

Multicoloured canopies were set up in front of the house and on the roof. The men all sat together and chatted outside, wearing freshly starched kurtas, and the women sat together inside, in their brightest saris. Sumithi led me inside with her, and we sat on the bed of one of the female relatives while the women spoke in Telugu and showed each other their flashy jewellery. Sumithi smiled and admired politely; I supposed their friends were used to the Gora women's strange jewel-free lifestyle.

Later, we were all called up to the roof. We passed Demos, who was on her way down, gorgeous in a plain white salwar kameez; she smiled at me and I blushed like I was meeting Bill Clinton. On the roof, we sat at rows of trestle tables that had been covered with sheets of white paper, and banana leaves were put in front of us. Uniformed bearers ladled out rice, biryani, curries, curd and sweets, and gave everyone a bottle of water. Every time a banana leaf started to look empty the bearers would cover it with more food. This was a real party, I thought, as Vijayam chatted in Telugu to the men around him. I like the way people in India feed each other as a sign of friendship and celebration, the way shared meals strengthen the bond of community. I couldn't help comparing the feast to the sad plates of raw vegetables and supermarket-bought dips that are often put out for guests at Australian parties.

After the meal, as we left, all the women received a gift bag containing bananas, a box of sweets and a plastic, silver-coloured Krishna.

When we arrived home, Vijayam told me that now was a good time to interview him and he invited me into his office. The interview involved me asking a couple of questions and him answering at length. The only break was at one point when I said, 'Excuse me, I think there's a bug in my kameez,' and he left the office in a very gentlemanly way while I fished around in my bra to remove the offending insect.

I told Vijayam that five years earlier everyone I had met in India seemed to want to talk about the Staines deaths, wanted to tell me how terrible they were, but now people were less interested. There was a feeling that this was something that had happened in the past.

Vijayam thought this was fair enough, in the sense that the incident had been an exception, an aberration; he didn't spell it out, but he gave the impression that Indian people couldn't keep beating themselves up over something that was remarkably unusual. 'People are welcoming in India. This kind of thing has happened so very rarely,' he said. In spite of possible undercurrents of resentment, he added, people generally appreciate all the good things that the missionaries did.

After my interview with Vijayam I discovered that I was in turn to be interviewed. Vijayam had phoned a friend called Sujatha, a reporter from the *Hindu* newspaper, and had told her an Australian writer was visiting Vijayawada. He assured me that Sujatha would write a positive story. 'She's like you, a very dynamic woman,' he told me. I wondered what 'dynamic' might turn out to be a euphemism for. Busty, as it happened.

I spoke to Sujatha at length. She was mainly interested in my first book, *Women of the Gobi*, about missionaries in China, and she was not afraid to be almost rude. When I explained that I was now writing a personal book rather than a dispassionate history, she bristled and asked, 'When there are so many different issues and facets of India, why are you just writing about your own experiences?'

'Because it's what I know,' I said.

Sujatha's photographer posed me in front of some pot plants, and then we drank coffee with Niyanta, Vijayam and Mithri, who chatted with Sujatha about the coming national elections and the state of the local schools. Vijayawada is quite famous for its educational facilities, they told me. Sujatha said that when she was first posted to Vijayawada she was told she must send her children to Sidhartha School, the most exclusive private school in town. But in the end she decided that the government school was better and that she didn't want her children to become snobs. 'They shouldn't only mix in one section of society,' she said.

I stood up to wash my coffee cup, and Sujatha nodded approvingly. She said she liked the way the Goras did housework for themselves and told me an anecdote about herself as a young journalist. When she first started work in the news office, the cleaners always moved the reporters' chairs around the room and didn't return them to their desks. She and her other young colleagues kept complaining, but the chairs kept moving. So they called a strike. 'We just said, "We don't have the right chairs so we're not going to work,"' she told me, putting on the voice of a petulant child.

While they stood around 'on strike', an older, senior journalist came into the room and asked what was going on.

'Our chairs aren't at our desks so we can't work,' Sujatha told him.

He said 'Oh' and quietly started moving the chairs to their desks.

The younger journalists fluttered around him, saying, 'Oh no, sir.'

But he smiled and said, 'It's not hard to move a chair.'

'We were all shamed,' Sujatha said.

That night Niyanta was taking me to the opening of a new block of buildings at the modern, private Kennedy International School. When he told Sujatha we were going, she laughed about how the school had recently added 'international' to its name but nothing had changed—the staff and students were still the same, she said.

When we arrived, masses of people were milling around. Thousands of plastic chairs were laid out facing the new building, and big video screens broadcast live pictures of the crowd. Everyone except Niyanta and me was beautifully dressed, just like the guests at the wedding. A red carpet from the gate to the new building was lined with schoolchildren holding bowls of petals, and the girls were wearing sequinned dresses. Larger-than-life-sized banners showed a young bearded priest wearing a saffron robe. He was a famous swami who was going to bless the building, Niyanta said. The children with the petals were waiting for him.

Apparently this is the normal practice, and it would be unusual for a new business undertaking not to be blessed with a Hindu ceremony and priest. I told Niyanta about a newspaper article I'd read about the new Tata Nano, a small, cheap car that had recently been launched in India. The first Nano off the assembly line had been taken to a series of important temples across the country to be blessed. 'Of course,' Niyanta said. ('Isn't it terrible?' one of my friends in Australia had said to me, after reading about the enthusiasm in India for the low-cost Tata Nano. She thought it would be bad for the environment if more Indians started driving. Yet my friend and her partner both own cars, which they drive to and from work every day.)

There was a great noise of shouting and bells when the swami arrived. A swell of people moved towards him as he and his entourage walked up the red carpet. I caught only a brief glimpse of him; he was surrounded by people drumming, holding flames over his head and ringing bells. Niyanta didn't sneer (none of the Goras ever do), but he did comment that it was rumoured to cost fifty thousand rupees (about a thousand dollars) to obtain the swami's services.

Niyanta and I agreed that we didn't much like crowds and parties like these. I had the impression that it was polite and politic for at least one member of the Gora family to make an appearance at this kind of shindig, but it wasn't much fun for them.

Niyanta suggested that on the way back we stop off at the shelter for street children run by the Atheist Centre in a more industrialised part of town. I suspect the decision to cross the tracks at this point, as a comparison to what we had just seen, was quite deliberate.

Down a narrow street, we drove past a high-walled auto-parts factory. Built up against its walls were mud huts, and milling around outside them were some dark, thin, dirty and desperately poor-looking people. Some were lying on string beds outside the huts. There were no streetlamps, and the only light came from truck headlights and occasional gas stoves and fires. I remember seeing these types of homes a lot in my childhood, but in my last couple of visits to India I'd thought they were disappearing as the middle class expanded. Trucks rattled past us, and the air coming through the car windows was hot and gritty and smelled like drains.

We passed through more side roads to a quieter area and reached the shelter, a modern building with empty fields on one side. I was surprised at how new and clean the building was, with a big communal area downstairs and a huge room crammed with bunk beds upstairs. There were electric lights and ceiling fans. It was about eight o'clock, and the building was empty save for a few staff members.

'The children are still out; they'll come later,' Niyanta said. 'Soon it will be full.' He told me that many of the children have jobs but have nowhere to go at night, and the shelter is partly about protecting them from sexual abuse. I was happy to see it while it was empty: I didn't want to take part in poverty tourism, gawking at the street kids like animals in a zoo. I think Niyanta knew this.

We drove home, passing the expensive Sidhartha School. During the night I dreamed about my young nephew and niece showing me pictures they had drawn.

The next morning everyone watched the news on television while we ate breakfast. Vijayam switched from a Telugu-language station to an English one so that I could understand the commentary. Banners read 'Cricket terror', and newsreaders were breathlessly reporting that the Sri Lankan cricket team had been attacked by gunmen in a commando-style ambush in Pakistan. The Goras shook their heads in sadness. 'We wonder how this will affect the election,' Vijayam said. National elections were only weeks away, and terrorism had been a hot topic in debates between politicians.

After breakfast I packed my bags and someone hailed an autorickshaw from the street. I was farewelled by all the family members, who urged me to return and bring Chris with me. I had told them he is a third-generation atheist, and they had been very impressed.

At the train station I bought a box of mango juice and chatted with a young Indian guy who asked where

I was from and wanted to talk about the bushfires near Melbourne. He said he lived in Detroit and was in India visiting family. I didn't tell him my name, but he must have looked for me on the seating chart posted on the carriage door, because after I found my seat he came and sat beside me and asked about the bushfires again. 'Katherine, how can this happen?' he said. 'Surely the government would have plans for this kind of thing in a hot country like Australia?'

I explained that Melbourne suffers from extreme heat for only a few days every year, and that it always seems to take people by surprise. 'I think this was the hottest day we'd ever had, and no-one had ever seen walls of fire move so big and fast,' I said.

I thought about my magnolia tree, which had been confused by the heat and dropped all its leaves, as if it was autumn. The woman sitting next to me had a string of jasmine in her hair, and the smell reminded me of home. Wherever that was.

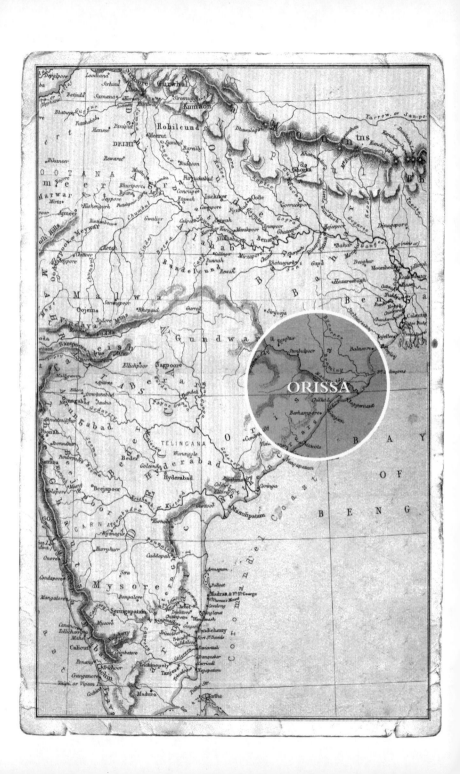

4

MISSIONARIES IN INDIA

There is a remarkably long tradition of non-belief in India. From about the sixth century to the fifteenth the Charvakas, also known as Lokayatas, espoused atheism and materialism. Few writings remain, but their most famous invocation translates along the lines of 'As long as you live happily, take a loan and drink ghee. After a body is reduced to ashes where will it come back from?' I liked the sound of that so much that I once set it as my Facebook status. 'Too much ghee and you'll be reduced to ashes sooner rather than later,' one wag commented.

Hinduism was a broad enough church in that period that it could contain the Charvakas, even though they called the writers of the Vedas 'buffoons' and accused Brahmin priests of being concerned only with money. Charvaka wasn't considered an orthodox school of Hinduism, but it was related; it was roughly on a par with Buddhism or Jainism. If the Hindu world was a family, the Charvaka philosophy was the rude old uncle who wasn't left alone with the kiddies but was still invited to Divali dinner.

Stranger even than the ancient association between atheism and Hinduism is the modern one. The man who founded the nationalist ideology Hindutva in the 1920s, Vinayak Damodar Savarkar, was an atheist who nevertheless saw Hindu identity as vitally tied up with Indian culture and loyalty to the fatherland. In his lifetime Savarkar was probably considered an eccentric distant relative within the wider Hindu family, but today he is patriarch to the influential cultural and political (and in some cases militant, even fascist) organisations that make up the Hindu nationalist Sangh Parivar, the 'family of associations'.

For months before my trip my parents had been forwarding emails to me from missionary organisations about refugee camps outside the city of Bhubaneswar, the capital of Orissa, the state where Graham Staines lived and died. Thousands of Christian converts from the southern Kandhamal district were being housed in the camps after having their homes burned down and being violently thrown out of their villages. I could imagine the mobs marching across the fields with torches. The violence had followed riots that started after the murder—for which Christians had been blamed—of an elderly Hindu priest called Laxmanananda, a proponent of Hindutva and an activist cow protector.

Cow liberation is a central project of the Bajrang Dal, one of the most strident of the Hindu organisations influenced by Hindutva. The group endorses and has links to the right-wing BJP, the second-biggest political party in India. It has campaigned to make cow slaughter illegal, as the cow is sacred to Hindus. It also campaigns against Christian missionaries, including Indian-born workers and organisations, and calls for mosques to be destroyed. It has been accused of many, many incidents of violence against Muslims and Christians and has been criticised by more moderate Hindu nationalist groups for bringing the movement into disrepute.

A former schoolmate from Hebron still living in India told me during my trip that communal violence and anger towards Christians in Orissa were tied up with politics, but he also claimed that the main tension was between Adivasi people, who used to be animists and had converted to Hinduism, and dalits, who were once on the lowest rung of Hinduism and had converted to Christianity. He added that the fires were being stoked by outsider high-caste Hindus. He also introduced me to the work of political scientist Pralay Kanungo. In a series of papers, Kanungo has charted the history of religion in Orissa in the twentieth century, pulling together the threads of politics, caste and belief. Until Independence, he says, there was little communal tension in Orissa. Christians did useful social work, but there were few conversions, and Hindus and Muslims lived comfortably together, sometimes synthesising their religious rituals and worship.

According to Kanungo, the Hindutva 'family of associations', the Sangh Parivar, quite deliberately sent Hindu missionaries into Orissa in the 1960s with a two-pronged campaign to counteract Christian activities. The first aim was to associate Krishna in his form as Jagannath, the lord of the universe—around whom Hinduism in Orissa centres—with the nationalist Hindutva ideology for Oriya-speaking Hindus. The second was to Hinduise Orissa's Adivasi people.

Laxmanananda, the priest whose murder had set off the most recent wave of communal violence, had had a lot of success in bringing Adivasi people over to Hinduism. In his work, Kanungo argued that the priest and other Hindu missionaries had taken advantage of traditional enmities between Adivasis and dalits—which had nothing to do with religion and were tied up with long-standing resentments over jobs, money and land rights—to demonise the dalits who had converted to Christianity. Hinduism was presented as the natural opposition to dalit Christianity. Kanungo said it wasn't surprising that dalits had converted to Christianity, as they were oppressed by the caste system and refused entry to temples. Christianity gave them some dignity. Upper-caste Hindus found this hard to stomach, he wrote, and it was in their interest to set the poor Adivasis against them.

Jagannath's image is everywhere in Orissa, usually hung with garlands. Unlike the major Hindu deities, who are usually portrayed in human or animal form, he is shown as a simple black rectangle of wood or stone with a smiling mouth and huge eyes. I hope I'm not offending anyone when I say he reminds me of SpongeBob SquarePants. The god's name is the source of the English word 'juggernaut', after the huge chariots that carry Jagannath through the streets once a year during the Ratha Yatra, the cart festival.

When my family visited Orissa in 1980 we were taken to a temple town (I think it must have been Koraput) to see the Jagannath temple and its carts. The wheels were as tall as my father. Our missionary friend Ray Valentine accompanied us and told us that during the Ratha Yatra devotees went into trances, threw themselves under the cartwheels and were crushed to death. It was demonic, he said.

I was horrified, imagining the cracking of a ribcage as a cart rolled across it. I looked closely at the wheels for traces of blood, but I couldn't see any splotches.

It's a story that foreigners have told for a long time. The British reported it in the eighteenth century, and Graham Staines wrote about the terrible cart festivals. But it seems that the stories are, well, only stories. It's more likely that occasionally people were accidentally crushed at the festivals—which still happens today—because of the huge crowds trying to get close to Jagannath.

Subhankar Ghosh, who was a close friend of Graham Staines, told me during my trip that he thought conditions for non-Hindus in India were worsening, that communal violence was on the rise. He said that richer urban families were getting ahead and that they didn't have any need for communalism, but he claimed that the huge majority was being left behind. 'Sometimes that can be manipulated into blaming other religions, and then the politicians benefit,' he said. He agreed when I suggested that the old certainties of status and caste were slowly breaking down, at least in urban areas, but he wasn't sure whether the rural majority would follow, or whether the divide would keep expanding. 'There are two Indias,' he said. It wasn't the first time I'd heard it.

Maoists, militant communists who operate in the country's eastern states, later claimed to have killed the swami Laxmanananda. According to Subhankar, Maoist insurgents often support Christians, especially the poor Adivasi ones. In one case they formed an armed guard and threatened to kill people if they interfered with Christian celebrations at Christmas.

Maoists don't hate foreign missionaries, he said; they just want to eradicate from the country 'all rich people and capitalists who earn by corrupt and unfair means'.

The Maoists, or Naxalites, aren't fans of foreign missionaries, but they aren't keen on Hindus either. They draw mixed responses from other Indians. The government has called them India's greatest security threat and accused them of forcing Adivasi people to work as their armed foot soldiers. The novelist Arundhati Roy has written compellingly in India's *Outlook* magazine about the abuses rained on India's Adivasi peoples and their complicated relationship with the Maoists. She says that in the 1970s nationalist Hindus started a drive to 'bring tribals back into the Hindu fold', which involved a campaign 'to denigrate tribal culture, induce self-hatred, and introduce Hinduism's great gift—caste'. Some Adivasis had come into the Hindu fold, but others had instead given their support to the Maoists. A picture has been painted of the Maoists as idealistic young rebels supporting Adivasi people against corrupt politicians and government-backed multinational mining companies who force them off their land. But there's no denying they have a lot of guns, and they haven't been afraid to use them.

When I asked Dr Vijayam at the Atheist Centre his thoughts on the reason for Graham Staines's murder, he said it was necessary to go all the way back into the history of India under the British. Before they arrived in the country there had been historically little hostility towards Christians. 'India is a mix of castes and races and invaders—people even say Christ was in Kashmir,' Vijayam told me. 'People celebrate each other's festivals. Hinduism pulls in other gods: it assimilates them. We welcome others, and it's not lip service; we really welcome them. That's not Hindu culture; that's Indian culture. With a few exceptions, there was always very little communalism.' But things changed with the British. 'When the Portuguese came, they settled in Goa; they married; they were influenced by the Indian way of life. But the British didn't want to settle. The British had guns. They started exploiting differences between people; it was divide and rule.' The British gave Christian missionaries land and other unfair advantages. 'They were like the cricket umpire always giving weight to the Christians,' he said, using a simile that any Indian would understand. 'When Indian people think about missionaries today, these issues are still in their minds.'

Vijayam said he couldn't comment on what the tipping point was in the Staines case, but he also didn't believe it was really a religious matter; he thought it was more likely to have been about local politics. He said that Christians are seen as constantly being involved in disputes over land, property and money, and that Indian Christians are well known for not declaring foreign money they receive. 'Of course the answer is that religions shouldn't be tax-free,' he said. 'It's not that we have an opposition to Christianity, but it's to do with these underhand activities ... so the thread of resentment is there. And this is from someone who has no horse in the race.'

Vijayam and his brother Niyanta told me a number of times that Christian missionaries did good works, that they had no problems with them, that they numbered missionaries among their friends. Niyanta used to give lifts on the back of his scooter to a Catholic priest from New Zealand, he said, and I pictured the priest's robes blowing out behind him as they sped through the streets.

Vijayam thought the philosophy—rather than the religion—of Jesus worth considering and said that Graham Staines was probably a good man but that the nature of missionary activity had been generally changing for the worse. Uneducated people in places like Orissa were being converted en masse without really understanding what they were doing. 'Global Christianity is losing its grip, and now people are in the numbers game. Christians have money. They're luring people and segregating them.'

I was a bit rattled by this. I couldn't imagine any missionaries I'd met behaving in this way. They all seemed very earnest, completely uninterested in converting 'rice Christians', and few missionaries I knew had any money to spare, let alone enough to bribe people into converting. I didn't say anything. I didn't believe what the missionaries believed, but I was surprised at how defensive I became when outsiders questioned their motives.

Not long before I had left for India, I had seen Elisabeth Valentine's face on the sidebar on my Facebook page under the heading 'People you may know'. She was older than I remembered, of course, and the hair that had been mousy brown when I knew her was now white and worn in two long plaits. But I recognised her straight away.

Elisabeth and her former husband, Ray Valentine, were Bible translators in Orissa when my family was living in Ooty, and their children studied at Hebron school. I visited the Valentines' village with my family when I was eight years old. I remember picking tamarinds and chasing monkeys with their children, and travelling in canoes on the river, and hearing shrews scrabbling on the roof of the house at night. The village men showed my father and brother how they made iron arrowheads for hunting and gave one to my brother, who still has it today. Elisabeth dosed out worm medicine to me after I told my mother I had an itchy bottom.

I sent Elisabeth a message. I was going to Orissa, I wrote, and I had vivid memories of staying in 'her' village but couldn't remember its name, or where exactly it was located. I wondered if she had known Graham Staines, and how she felt about his death.

I sent her a picture, a slide from my parents' collection that I had scanned, showing her, Ray and my mother lined up in front of their jeep on a dusty jungle track. When I was a child I thought of Elisabeth as old, mainly because she wore her hair back in a bun like a grandmother, but the slide showed a tall, strong-looking, attractive woman in her thirties.

Elisabeth responded, telling me to call her Liz ('less stuffy') and asking after my family. She lived in Perth with her new husband, she said. He was, like me, a writer and a 'non-theist humanist'. She noted that the slide I'd sent had been flipped, as the lungi she wore in the picture was fastened on the wrong side. I was impressed that she remembered a detail like that.

The village was called Sujanakota, Liz said. It was actually on the Andhra Pradesh side of the state border, but to get there they'd had to travel by jeep through parts of Orissa. The Valmiki people, whose language she and Ray studied and translated, were animists, though during the 1970s she saw men who'd been to school outside the village adopting Hindu ideas and ceremonies. Hindu nationalism had not been a threat to Christians, as far as she knew.

She didn't think she had met Graham in India, but she had been shocked when she'd heard about his death. That 'the two young boys in particular were subjected to that, despite Indians having such a soft spot for children' affected her. She remembered seeing

Gladys on television and being impressed by her 'strong will to forgive'.

During my trip, as I travelled through Orissa and thought about missionary life there, I wondered what had led Liz and Ray to India, and whether they had felt safe. Were their children happy in the village, and did they regret having to send them off to boarding school? I wanted to ask Liz about these matters, but I wasn't sure how to pose the questions that most interested me. It was clear that her beliefs about Christianity and missionary work had shifted to some extent over the years, and I wondered why. On her Facebook page, under the 'Religion' heading she had written 'personal'. I decided to ask about it anyway.

Liz was generous and gracious in her detailed reply. She and Ray moved to India in November 1968 after training in linguistics, and they settled in Sujanakota to analyse the local language—which had yet to be written down—and translate the New Testament into it. Liz didn't say this, but it was clear from published material online that their work remains the major contribution to understanding of the language.

Liz studied anthropology at Sydney University, she wrote, 'and I became very sensitive to the idea that if missionaries go to other cultures they need to be careful not to try and force cultural changes, because if you take away something which has served a culture very well for centuries you really should have something that serves just as well or better—so it's wisest not to tamper with things'.

Her memories were almost all positive. She enjoyed village life, which was in some ways like a fifteen-year camping trip. The houses were built from the earth, the scenery was beautiful, the food was fresh. She remembered walking into the jungle to pick mangoes, nursing a stray dog back to health ('he remained our faithful dog until a leopard killed and ate him one mango season'), attending weddings and coming-of-age ceremonies, enjoying local dances and music.

The people the Valentines lived with were hospitable and straightforward: 'When they were sad they were sad, when they were happy they were happy, when they were angry they were angry … They did not put on airs like many people I knew in the Western world; they did not put on masks, so to speak, to pretend to be better people than they were, like evangelical Christians were expected to back home.' She believed they had been accepted in the community. They grew close to some of the families in the village. 'When you live as part of a community such as we did in Sujanakota, and experience other cultures yourself, you get to know and love people of all types and backgrounds, and it is unavoidable … to accept that there are people of great integrity in all cultures.'

Overall, Liz believed that she and Ray were a positive influence on the local villagers. By eating meat and vegetables while she was pregnant with no ill effects, she set an example to the village women who believed this would harm the baby. She was able to offer medical help. She taught some women to read and guided them to teach others. She travelled to a big city hospital with one woman to be her nursemaid when the woman had a caesarean—there were jobs the hospital nurses would not do because of caste taboos. With money from aid agencies, Ray helped the men to build a literacy house, a furnace for baking and better nets for fishing. People in the village gained a pride in their language when books became available.

Liz never feared for her safety in the village. When she travelled, there were occasional incidents of harassment from men, 'but that could have happened anywhere, and is not representative of India specifically'. The only times she was afraid was when her eldest son was sick and Ray had to take him to hospital some distance away: 'It was very frightening waiting to see whether he would come back alive and well.' On another occasion their jeep had broken down and Ray had to take their younger son to hospital by boat after he broke his leg.

The Valentine children also enjoyed village life—like the Staines children, Liz's daughter spoke mainly the local language in her pre-school years—and the hardest aspect of being in India was sending the children to boarding school. 'It broke Ray's heart for a while there,' Liz wrote. She thought that, after some initial difficulties in adjusting, the children had been mainly happy at school, and they exchanged regular letters.

During their last two years in India, while she was preparing the New Testament for printing, Liz spent all of her time in Ooty, typing up her work and spending weekends with the children. Ray went back and forth between Ooty and the village. I remember them living at the missionary guesthouse in Ooty; I would hear the tapping of the typewriter when I went over to play with their daughter and can picture the great piles of paper next to it.

Finally, Liz tackled, without answering fully, my question about whether her beliefs had changed. She said that she had never believed in coercing people into faith.

I have a great dislike of people 'counting converts', or of being so over-possessed with 'winning souls' that that is all they can think of. I have seen missionaries, but also people who run churches at home in Australia, and ordinary adherents, who have become obsessive to the extent that everything has to be couched in religious jargon, that their views are expressed as 'the' right ones, making everyone else an 'outsider', 'not saved', etc.

Liz wanted to be careful in how she expressed her thoughts about missionaries. 'At times in history there have been missionaries who have acted without adequate sensitivity towards the people they have believed they were serving, and some are known to have acted without proper understanding, and in some cases even cruelly,' she wrote. 'There are others who have lived lives of utmost integrity wherever they were, and many medical missionaries could be included among them, I suspect.' She didn't agree with people who like to blame missionaries for all the harm done to other cultures. Government administrators, traders and social workers have been just as intrusive, if not more so, she thought.

She did not regret what she and Ray did, or how they did it. 'People do as they do at a given time on the basis of their lights at that time; I accept that for myself, as well as for others.'

Liz did not want her beliefs to be categorised; she thought people who strongly identify with a particular religion often have 'blinkers on that prevent them hearing, seeing, interpreting, responding to other valid truths'. Respect and tolerance between religions are important, she wrote; people should be free to make their own choices about these things.

I read and re-read Liz's email. I understood her ambivalence about missionaries completely. It comforted me to know that there were other people who felt this way.

Over the past few decades a number of Indian states, including Orissa, have introduced or strengthened anti-conversion legislation, usually giving the laws Orwellian names like 'Freedom of Religion Bill'. In some states it's now a jailable offence for anyone to claim that someone would be better off following a different religion. A religious group offering education or health care is in danger of being fined for giving 'inducements'. Attempts to convert women, children and 'depressed classes' (Adivasis or dalits) carry higher fines, as these are seen as groups who can be easily manipulated.

Christian, Islamic and human rights groups have argued that the laws are in fact in direct opposition to freedom of religion. An interesting response was made by Percival Fernandez, the Catholic bishop of Mumbai, who suggested to AsiaNews that legislators should stop wasting time on anti-conversion laws and instead use their 'precious time to plan and execute projects that get drinking water, decent housing, daily affordable bread and primary education to the millions who are deprived of these basic requirements for which they have a right'.

At the time of writing, no foreign missionaries have been charged under the laws—the negative publicity overseas would perhaps be a problem—but plenty of Indian Christians have been jailed and fined on what looks like pretty flimsy evidence. In a country where more than eighty per cent of the population are Hindu and only two per cent claim to be Christian, it's hard to know why the Hindutva ideologues are so threatened by minority religions that they need to be locking up their adherents. Looking at these figures, I can't help but think there is a parallel to be drawn with the United States. There, about eighty per cent of the population call themselves Christian, and yet far-right fundamentalists fret about the dangers posed to their way of life by the less than one per cent of the population that is Muslim. In both cases, I suspect the impulse is political, not religious.

In fact, India at the start of the twenty-first century feels a bit like the United States of the twentieth century. Most people wouldn't think of India as a young country; indeed, to most foreigners, the lure of India is all about its ancient culture. But since the Indian market was opened up in the early 1990s the economy has surged, and a whole fresh, enthusiastic new middle class has emerged. Globalisation has been good to India, and mass consumer culture is changing the country, for better or for worse.

In *Time* magazine in late 2010, Fareed Zakaria wrote about the 'fatalism and socialist lethargy' of India in the 1970s, and how he and other Indians looked instead to the optimism of the American Dream. But on a recent trip to India, he said, 'it's as if the world has been turned upside down. Indians are brimming with hope and faith in the future. After centuries of stagnation, their economy is on the move, fuelling animal spirits and ambition. The whole country feels as if it has been unlocked.'

With all the new money has come a kind of shallow materialism. Indian films and television celebrate financial success and celebrity as the most important goals in life. And who am I to wander in from my comfortable life in Australia and condemn this? Would anyone prefer to return to the India of the 1970s, when people were dying of starvation in the streets of Kolkata?

But I can't forget the people who told me that there are two Indias, moving further apart. There are big chunks of India that remain locked out of the new prosperity while seeing the flashing neon signs of it all around them. Others are actively oppressed by the open economy, like the Adivasis who have been displaced and exploited by multinational mining companies. As far as I can see, these real, understandable resentments will continue to be manipulated by people who preach religious intolerance for political gain, the kinds of people who applauded the killing of Graham Staines and his boys.

Before I left Australia, I watched a fundraising DVD produced by a mission organisation that I hoped would help me to visit the Christian refugee camps in Orissa. The DVD contained a series of stories about miracles God had performed in the state. In one story, the narrator said that many people who lived in a certain village had become Christians and had thrown away all their Hindu charms and amulets because Jesus had freed them from superstition. The villagers still believed the charms had power, but they now believed it was the wrong kind of power. An old man was interviewed, and he explained that when the Hindu amulets had been thrown away onto the branches of a tree outside the village, the evil spirits in them had caused the branches to wither. The Hindu charms and amulets had looked just like the necklaces and medallions for sale at the Saint Thomas shrine in Chennai.

Another segment recounted the story of an entire village in Orissa that had apparently been converted to Christianity, with more than five hundred people baptised in the river at the same time. 'They've demolished the Hindu temple and built a church,' the voiceover said. I thought it was pretty bad form for the narrator to be referring gleefully to the demolition of a temple, as, in the context of communal violence in India, this is a very sore point. One of the most contentious issues in the country since the rise of Hindu nationalism has been over a patch of land in the town of Ayodhya, in Uttar Pradesh. A Muslim place of worship, the Babri Mosque, was built on the site in 1528 by the Mughals, and many Hindus believe an older shrine to Lord Rama was destroyed in the process. Since 1949 endless court cases and political fights have raged over the issue of who owns the sacred ground, and in 1992 a riot—which some believe was started by the Bajrang Dal—destroyed the mosque. About two thousand people died in resulting riots across India. Whether this was a grassroots upwelling of Hindu feeling or a cynically engineered political stunt is still being argued. Either way, whoever wrote the commentary for the mission organisation's DVD could perhaps have chosen their words more carefully.

In 2009 three different Christians, friends of mine or of my parents, sent me a link to the same opinion piece from the *London Times* in which Matthew Parris argued that, even though he was an atheist, his experiences in Africa had convinced him that Christianity was a force for good. Giving people the opportunity to convert to Christianity was the best way to improve lives, he said. People sent me the article because they thought I would agree with it; they knew I had written sympathetically about missionaries in the past. I thanked them, but they were wrong. I actually thought that debt relief and investment and microloans to women and clean water and antimalarials and condoms might be the best ways to start improving the lives of the world's poor. I still do. But in the article Parris also discussed Christian converts reclaiming dignity.

Anxiety—fear of evil spirits, of ancestors, of nature and the wild, of a tribal hierarchy, of quite everyday things—strikes deep into the whole structure of rural African thought. Every man has his place and, call it fear or respect, a great weight grinds down the individual spirit, stunting curiosity. People won't take the initiative, won't take things into their own hands or on their own shoulders.

...

Christianity, post-Reformation and post-Luther, with its teaching of a direct, personal, two-way link between the individual and God, unmediated by the collective, and unsubordinate to any other human being, smashes straight through the philosophical/spiritual framework I've just described. It offers something to hold on to to those anxious to cast off a crushing tribal groupthink. That is why and how it liberates.

Parris may have been simplistic and condescending about it, but maybe he had a point. If I could believe that Christianity might be a positive force for the Adivasis and dalits of Orissa, then I could believe that Graham Staines was doing a good thing for them and that his death was, perhaps, a straightforward, uncomplicated tragedy. It's certainly what I want to believe.

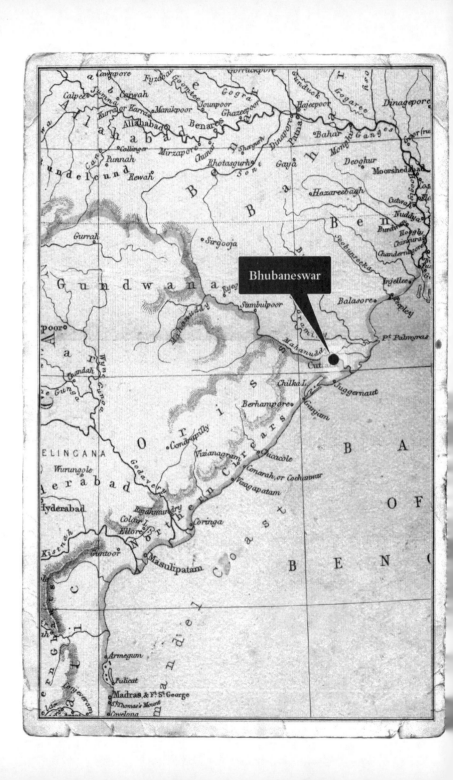

5

BHUBANESWAR

I alighted from the train early in the morning in Bhubaneswar, the capital of Orissa, where I was going to spend a night before travelling on to Baripada, the town where Graham Staines had lived and worked. I had visited Bhubaneswar once before, only a few months earlier, when I researched Orissa for Lonely Planet's India guidebook. I had seen pretty much every hotel in town, and I knew that most of the cheaper ones were grottier than average and not very friendly to foreign travellers. I thought that as I was in town only for one night, therefore, I could justify some air-conditioning. I caught an autorickshaw away from the smelly, noisy centre to the Ginger Hotel, on the green outer edge of town.

Air-conditioning may not seem like a huge luxury to many travellers, especially in such a hot part of the world, and Ginger is hardly a five-star hotel. I'm sure many travel writers stay at much nicer places. But, aside from being pretty skint, I grew up in India with parents who earned Indian wages, and the way we lived then still informs the way I travel today. I catch local buses rather than take taxis whenever I can, and usually my only prerequisites for the hotels I stay in are basic cleanliness, a ceiling fan and a working lock on the door.

On my previous trip I'd been dropped off at Ginger by Tutu, a local tour guide who had helped me to travel around the tribal areas in the south of the state. We'd taken some long car trips together—another luxury I'd struggled with—and I'd asked him about communal violence in Orissa and the persecution of Christians. Tutu was a Hindu, but he wasn't particularly devout. He'd said the violence was annoying for him, because he couldn't take tourists into the affected areas. He told me that it hadn't been as bad as the newspapers had made out, and that it wasn't really about religion: people just wanted the Christians' land. He implied that the Christians had come by their land unfairly, that perhaps the violence was understandable. He laughed at the idea of thousands of Christians being displaced and said it wasn't nearly that number.

I had been reading the English-language papers in Orissa and had seen only a few short reports about the violence. The writers were careful not to take sides, and in fact there had been interviews published with Hindu leaders who said that the violence had actually been aimed at Hindus, by Christians. It wasn't until later, when I reached Kolkata, that I had read any newspaper reports, let alone opinion pieces, that accepted that Christians had been targeted.

I remembered Ginger's receptionist, an open-faced young man with a ponytail whose name tag said 'Arun', and he recognised me. 'So you have returned to Bhubaneswar,' he said, smiling and possibly a little surprised, while he signed me in.

The lobby was quiet, with just one young couple sitting in the attached cafe, part of an India-wide chain called Cafe Coffee Day. The man and the woman were both wearing jeans, and they talked softly and intensely. Arun had told me before that unmarried couples would come in, order the cheapest drink on the menu and sit there for hours, because they were unlikely to be seen by their parents or their parents' friends. Going on an unchaperoned date could still get you into a lot of trouble, even in educated and well-off circles.

Arun seemed keen to chat and told me I needed to see the ancient Hindu temples of Bhubaneswar. I'd explored them on my last visit; they're covered with elaborately carved figures from Hindu mythology. Once again I'd spotted figures that looked like mermaids: representations of Nagarani, the snake goddess. No other foreign travellers had been on the tour, but tourists from all over India had come to see the temples. The other tourists and I had spoken to each other in English.

'I've seen the temples, but I'm interested in what Hinduism is like today,' I said to Arun. 'What do you think of this Hindutva movement? Is it getting stronger?'

Arun shook his head. 'None of my friends are following this way,' he said. 'I tell you, I have a Muslim friend and I went to the mosque with him, and he goes to the temple with me. Nobody is interested in these fanatics.' He told me that all the young people he knew were working hard and concentrating on making money. There was a lot of money to be earned in India these days, he said, and everyone was getting richer, and he wanted to be part of it. He smiled. He wasn't embarrassed or ashamed.

He agreed when I said life seemed to be changing fast in India. I asked him if things were changing for everyone, the bulk of Indians.

'Oh no, just ten, fifteen per cent,' he said. He shrugged, as if to say 'What can you do?' 'You're from Australia,' he said, looking at my passport. 'We all know Australia from the cricket!'

I don't know anything about cricket, but I was aware that the Australian team regularly plays in India and I had a vague idea that Ricky Ponting had started up some kind of children's charity there. And I remembered a newspaper story about Shane Warne taking a suitcase full of canned baked beans to India with him because he didn't like foreign food.

'Ricky Ponting loves India,' I said, off the top of my head.

Arun smiled broadly. 'Ricky Ponting is very good.'

I didn't go and look at the temples again. The air outside the hotel was insanely hot. Instead, I showered, washed my clothes, plugged my phone and laptop into the wall and stayed inside for the whole day. I needed to literally and figuratively recharge my batteries. I would sit in the cafe and take advantage of the free wifi, I thought, and read a book.

The Black-Eyed Peas' 'My Humps' was playing in the cafe when I arrived an hour or so later. I ordered a chicken sandwich and a milkshake, which cost only marginally less than they would have at a cafe in Australia. I had eaten a lot of dosai and vegetable curries over the past couple of weeks, and I was starting to crave something bland, processed and protein-rich. I sat down in a comfy seat by a low table with my laptop, phone and iPod. The next song to play was the Pussycat Dolls' 'Don't Cha'.

The cafe was clean and air-conditioned. A couple of other foreigners sat with their laptops, but most of the customers were well-dressed, English-speaking young Indians lingering over a single drink. After my conversation with Arun I couldn't help noticing the young couples, who I imagined were looking around furtively, scared of being caught sharing a milkshake. I didn't see anyone holding hands.

One of my classmates from Hebron School, Parvathy, came from a Hindu family, and I knew her older brother had entered an arranged marriage; this was still the norm in India at the time. A couple of years after we left school, when I heard that Parvathy was getting married, I assumed she had also followed the traditional route. I probably felt a bit sorry for her.

On my previous trip to the south I had visited her in her home town of Bangalore, where she had returned after her recent divorce. Her husband had been abusive, she said. I asked somewhat patronisingly about the difficulties of arranged marriages, and she laughed and said, 'It was a love match'. The phrase is used in conversation and newspaper articles in India when noting the rise of such marriages. Parvathy had met her husband in college and had married him in spite of her family's disapproval. She had been one of those young people courting on the sly.

She said she had pursued a relationship her parents wouldn't like because she felt disconnected from them and their beliefs. 'I did it for liberation but unfortunately it was with the wrong person,' she wrote to me later. 'I found true liberation in my separation. Now I find my happiness in small ways.'

Parvathy's older brother was still happy in his arranged marriage, but her younger siblings had mostly married for love. A couple of them had converted to Christianity, and one had even married a foreigner, which had been difficult for their parents to accept. Parvathy saw herself as spiritual rather than religious. She didn't regularly attend any kind of worship, she told me, but she still prayed. I didn't ask who she prayed to.

I ate my lunch and then emailed Chris, telling him that I was a little nervous about my trip to Baripada. I would be arriving at night, on my own, in a town I didn't know. I would have to explain myself to Christians who would be disappointed in me. Indians generally might be tolerant of other beliefs, but Indian evangelicals are the same as evangelicals everywhere: they would be pleasant to me but there would be a distance, and they would believe, in the end, that I was going to hell. I was filled with a vague anxiety.

While I was typing my phone rang. It was my mother. 'I had a dream that you died in India,' she said, slightly more cheerfully than I might have liked. 'Chris wanted you to have an atheist funeral, and we weren't sure what you would've wanted.'

I assumed my mother had been more rattled by my positive experiences at the Atheist Centre, which I had described to her in an email, than she cared to admit.

'Do I have to have a funeral?' I said. 'I don't want songs or sermons; you can just get together and talk about me—and try to say nice things.'

'Okay,' she said.

We didn't talk for much longer.

I went back to my email and told Chris about the phone call. 'If you really want music at my funeral, play Tom Waits's "Shiver Me Timbers",' I wrote. I had been listening to the song on my iPod, and the image of the sailor in the crow's nest disappearing out to sea and into the unknown appealed to me.

Chris emailed back straightaway. 'When I die I want them to play "Mah Na Mah Na" at my funeral. From then on when anyone who was there hears "Mah Na Mah Na" they'll feel a little sad … bittersweet.'

I wasn't cheered up much. The fact that someone was thinking about my death at the same time that I felt worried and isolated made me even more anxious. Were my mother and I both sensing something?

And when I phrased it like that, in my head, I realised how superstitious and fatalistic the thought was. I didn't, for a moment, believe in that kind of thinking. 'It's understandable that my mum might have that dream when I'm heading out to a fairly remote place where an Australian was killed, and I'd emailed her about how I liked the atheists,' I wrote to Chris. 'And it's understandable that I'm nervous too, and even slightly worried about my safety, just from being alone and missing my peeps.'

He wrote back, 'Or maybe you could play Cameo's "Candy" at my funeral. And everyone could wear bright-red codpieces.' He was just making fun of me now.

Another message popped into my inbox. It was from Dr Vijayam, and it contained the text of Sujatha's article about me, which had been published in the *Hindu*. While the topics covered in the article were those we had discussed, the wording of the quotes attributed to me was mostly unfamiliar. It reminded me of an article written by a work experience student I had once supervised when I was a newspaper journalist; I had been about to submit the article to the editor, and I praised the student for the lively quotes he had gleaned from his subject.

'Oh, I couldn't reach him so I made them up,' he had told me, completely unapologetically.

....

She has managed to keep away from the genre that gets caught up in the monotony of daily grind, and in the bargain, she has gained advantage of not losing track of what keeps life fresh, fun and interesting.

Kate James, a writer from Melbourne in Australia is joie de vivre personified. Having lived in India for eight years in the 1980s until she was 15, and her parents working as teachers at Hebron School, an international school in Ooty, Kate has had ample scope to savour quite a slice of the delicious India …

When she returned to Australia, she pursued journalism and worked for different papers. 'Whenever I had enough time and money I would travel back to India bringing friends with me. I barely realized that I had become a bit of a tour guide.'

For Kate, Singapore is the happiest place in the world. Pray why? 'It is the place where I change my plane, between India and Australia. So, no matter which direction I am going, I am on my way home,' she chuckles.

A few years ago, the 36-year-old Australian opted for a career change and became Editor for Lonely Planet, a Melbourne-based company that produces travel guides to almost every place in the world. 'It was then that I wrote my first book *Women of the Gobi* which talks about my journey through northwest China in 2005 in the footsteps of three English women who crossed the Gobi desert in the 1920s.'

Kate was so fascinated by the tale of the trio that she decided to re-visit the places and blend her own experiences with that of theirs in her book. 'China was a fascinating place to visit. I had prepared myself to confront a very authoritarian society. But in many ways, it felt similar to other parts of Asia. Rapid technological changes and people opening up to the idea of welcoming foreigners came as pleasant surprises,' she recounts.

Referring to the Chinese stories of the Monkey King, which she had seen on television in Australia, she says: 'I was happy to find pictures and statues of the Monkey King and other characters from the stories. It reminded me of Hanuman of the Indian mythology.'

As a guide writer to the West Bengal and Orissa chapters of Lonely Planet's guide to India, Kate travelled across the length and breadth of the two states checking out hotels and restaurants and bus stations and tourist sights. When she was in Kolkata, she received an email from Australian Council, a government agency, informing that it was ready to fund her research and she could also write her own book about her travels in India. 'I am already on the job. I'll touch upon a lot of subjects and the book will be based on my personal experiences.'

Toss a suggestion to extend her horizons and she is quick to answer: 'I can be more honest while dealing with my own emotions rather than pretending to be an authority on the stupendous and rich India.'

....

She might not have entirely captured the way I talked, but Sujatha didn't get anything very wrong, and the article cheered me up. I couldn't be moping: I was joie de vivre personified!

The television station in Cafe Coffee Day was tuned to TimesNow, an English-language news station. It seemed more sensationalist than the news channel I usually watch, CNN-IBN (which I prefer mainly because it features Australian television journalist Stan Grant, who has become something of an imaginary friend to me when I'm on the road). Two stories dominated the news cycle over the day. The first ran under the banner 'Cricket terror': the attack on the Sri Lankan cricket team in Pakistan and pictures of the aftermath were rehashed over and over. An Indian journalist who looked and dressed remarkably like US Fox News commentator Sean Hannity berated his various guests over the terrible state of security in Pakistan. His aim seemed to be to inflame the situation as much as possible. The second story used the headline 'Stop the auction now'. Items that had belonged to Mahatma Gandhi—a bowl, a pair of glasses, sandals—were being sold at auction in New York. Hannity-ji said they should instead be returned to the Indian government by their owner, a US collector. It was hard to tell which of the two stories had outraged him more.

I have often told friends about the explosives factory in Wellington with the statue of the famously non-violent Gandhi outside. Like my father, who first pointed it out, I think it laughably ironic. But in India, nobody ever understands my point, or they think it's a stupid point. Once, after I told the story to a tailor in Mamallapuram, he took my hand and showed me how each of my fingers was different. It was the same with people, he said. They all had different jobs to do in life, and different ways of doing things, but if they did their jobs right then everything worked together properly. It was appropriate, he was saying, that some people should build explosives factories and others fight against them. That was the way the world worked.

I once saw the blood-stained dhoti that Gandhi was wearing when he was shot dead. It is preserved in a glass case in the only air-conditioned room in the Gandhi Memorial in Madurai. I was the only person there, walking around the quiet, humid building lined with photos and stories. I don't think Gandhi's death is terribly important to most Indians; it is his life that is remembered. It's a shame that the same can't be said for Graham Staines.

I was reading the online archives of Indian magazines when an email popped into my inbox. It was from Subhankar Ghosh, a botany professor and an old friend of Graham Staines. He had been in Manoharpur on the night of the deaths, and along with his wife, Mira, he now heads up the leprosy mission in Baripada. He confirmed that someone would pick me up at the Baripada train station the following evening. I was going to spend some time with the Christians.

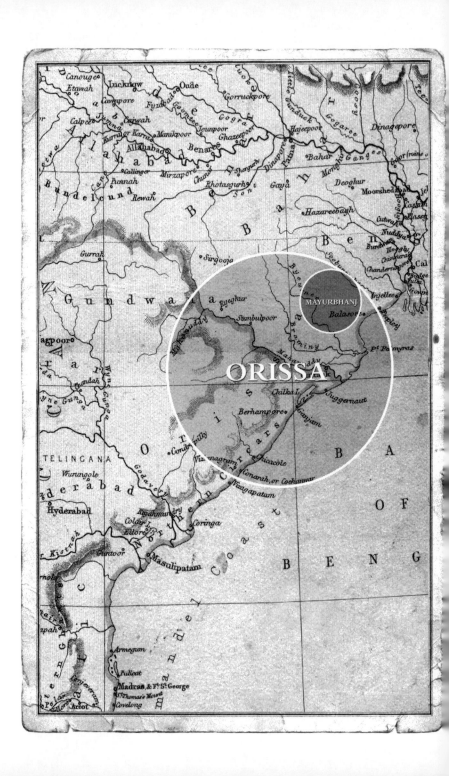

6

MAYURBHANJ

Josia, a young man in the early stages of leprosy, was the answer Graham Staines always gave when asked why he had gone to India. A missionary called Vera Stevens visited Beaudesert Baptist Church when Graham was in his early twenties. She presented a slide show about missionary activity in Orissa, and one picture showed Josia. Graham claimed to have been haunted by the fear in the man's eyes. He had gone home and read the gospel of Mark and cried when he reached the following passage: 'So [Jesus] traveled throughout Galilee, preaching in their synagogues and driving out demons. A man with leprosy came to him and begged him on his knees, "If you are willing, you can make me clean." Jesus was indignant. He reached out his hand and touched the man. "I am willing," he said. "Be clean!" Immediately the leprosy left him, and he was cleansed.'

At that point Graham was already studying at the Queensland Bible Institute with the aim of becoming a missionary. Now he knew where he should go. He applied to the Evangelical Missionary Society in Mayurbhanj and arrived in India in January 1965, just before his twenty-fourth birthday. He lived there for the rest of his life.

Graham was born in 1941 in Palmwoods, Queensland. He had a devout mother and a periodically alcoholic father. *Burnt Alive*, a book that was rushed out by a Christian publisher in Mumbai within a couple of months of Graham's and his sons' deaths, is a mishmash of eyewitness accounts of the incident, quotes about Graham and the boys from people who knew them in Baripada, reproduced sections of a 1995 centennial history of the Christian work in the town, reprinted editorials from Indian magazines and newspapers, and a straight-up gospel message. It also gives a history of Graham's early years in India. Based in the remote town of Baripada, in Mayurbhanj district, he worked for a small evangelical mission that treated and rehabilitated people with leprosy. Initially, very few buildings had electricity, and in the evenings Graham studied Oriya, the language spoken across the state, by the light of a lantern. He arranged to have electricity connected and later wrote home, 'The wiring is finished, but I've found a few things not right, like earthing.' Judging by how wiring is usually rigged up in India, this comment was either delightfully naive or hilariously deadpan. 'There was no fuse on the power point circuit,' he added, in apparent surprise.

In those early days, much of Graham's time was spent fixing the mission car, a 1932 Ford (called Henry, of course, and known by that name throughout the district) that had been rebuilt from the ground up by a previous missionary. He wrote to his brothers with details of Henry's various complaints and his repair methods. In between language classes he did other odd jobs, as well as teaching Bible lessons and getting to know the local Christians.

People knew Graham as a practical man, a committed Christian and also a gifted administrator. He worked hard to learn Oriya and within a few years could also communicate in Santali and Ho, local Adivasi languages. He took over management of the mission in 1983, the same year in which he married Gladys Weatherhead, a nurse from Queensland who had visited Baripada with a Christian team a couple of years earlier. Esther was born in 1986, followed by Philip and Timothy; they were three white-blonde children who spoke and sang in Oriya and played with the local children.

At the time of Graham's death, he and his family were the only foreigners still working for the mission in India, and he had become the mission superintendent. In a newsletter in the mid-1990s, the Australian-based president of the mission had written:

....

Mayurbhanj Mission needs a person who can:
  Administer the whole work,
  Attend to all the needs of the Leprosy Home
      and all the patients,
  Arbitrate for people,
  Counsel people in all conceivable situations,
  Speak Oriya and Santhal fluently,
  Advise in agriculture,
  Understand animal husbandry,
  Build,
  Maintain vehicles,
  Train leaders,
  Function on a shoestring budget,
  Accept the ridicule of disgruntled, professing
      Christians,
  Be a guardian of mission helpers,
  And fit in time to be a caring husband and
      father.

....

The kicker, of course, was the last line: 'And we already have him (Graham Staines) for which we are most thankful to his Lord and ours.'

The tradition of the 'jungle camp' started long before Graham went to live in Baripada, but he took to it straightaway. It involved travelling to small, isolated villages, where at least a few Christians lived, and carrying out a series of meetings with Bible teaching and Christian music. The missionaries and Christians from surrounding areas showed slides and distributed healthcare tips and lessons in hygiene. The main aim wasn't proselytism, but it was always hoped that non-Christian villagers would show an interest in the faith. When Graham first arrived in Baripada the other missionaries were all women who were unwilling or unable to travel long distances into the jungle on their own, but Graham travelled for hours on back roads to reach remote villages.

One of these villages, about a five-hour drive from Baripada, was Manoharpur. It was home to around a hundred and fifty families of Santal tribespeople, who had a mix of Hindu and animist beliefs and traditions that revolved around their relationship with the soil. Graham and some local Christians first visited the village in 1978, preaching and showing film strips about Christianity. By 1999 the jungle camp was a regular four-day event in the village, and about twenty-two families called themselves Christian.

In the late 1990s there was some tension between the Christians and other villagers who said the Christians had offended against local customs by continuing to tend their crops during a time when the earth was traditionally left fallow, as Mother Earth was said to be menstruating. This was considered serious desecration. In addition, Christians were seen to be getting ahead of the other villagers financially; there were rumours that they were receiving money from the missionaries. In fact, it seems that the Christians were mainly benefiting in practical ways because they no longer drank alcohol or sacrificed animals to appease evil spirits.

On 20 January 1999, Graham travelled to Manoharpur with his two sons, a visiting Australian pastor called Gilbert Venz, Graham's old friend and mission supporter Subhankar Ghosh, four local evangelists, a driver and a cook.

According to the findings of the official investigation, the trouble started at about eleven o'clock on the third night, 22 January. Graham, Philip and Timothy were asleep in the back of their jeep, while the other visitors were staying in the homes of Christian villagers. A crowd of about thirty-five men—only a few of them turned out to be Manoharpur villagers—appeared from the fields, surrounded the vehicle and started banging on it with lathis, or long sticks, and other implements. They chanted, apparently, though there was some confusion as to what they said. A few of the men broke off from the group to guard the nearby houses and prevent anyone from getting out.

The windows of the jeep were broken. Villagers who were trapped in their houses or hiding nearby said they heard a child's screams. People in the crowd grabbed the hay that Graham had placed on the jeep's roof for insulation against the cold night air and threw it inside the vehicle, setting fire to it with flaming torches. The men stabbed at Graham and the boys with trishuls.

Then they stood around the jeep as it burned, beating back anyone who tried to get close. After about half an hour three loud whistles were sounded, and the mob disappeared into the night.

When the villagers came out and found the remains in the morning, they could see that Graham had died holding his boys close to him.

According to the Wadhwa Commission, the official judicial inquiry whose findings were released six months later, the mob had been led by a man known as Dara Singh, who was not a local but had moved to Orissa from Uttar Pradesh. He had encouraged the mob, the commission found, by saying, 'Let us go and assault the Christian missionaries who have come to Manoharpur as they are indulging in conversion of innocent tribals to Christianity and are spoiling our religion and culture.' Singh already had a criminal record. In addition to theft of clothes and money from local traders, he had also been charged a number of times with religiously motivated cattle rustling. He and a few followers had hijacked Muslim cattle trucks destined for the slaughter yard, beating up the drivers, liberating the cows and distributing them to grateful villagers.

A number of eyewitnesses to the murders in Manoharpur claimed that they had heard the mob chant 'Long live the Bajrang Dal.' The Wadhwa Commission noted this but also said there was no evidence that the strident Hindu group, which is influenced by Hindutva, had orchestrated the violence.

The commission's findings were criticised by human rights groups. A 1999 report by the Asia Pacific Human Rights Network accused it of both investigative incompetence and political whitewashing: 'At a time when the BJP is attempting to move into the political mainstream, the Commission's Report seeks to assuage fears of religious minorities and tolerant Hindus that the BJP is unable or unwilling to control militant groups such as Bajrang Dal.' The Bajrang Dal said that it had nothing to do with Dara Singh. On the other hand, a spokesperson suggested, Graham Staines had had it coming, and you couldn't blame young people for wanting to defend their culture and religion.

An article in *India Today* published soon after the commission had brought down its verdict asked the questions that are still being argued over today: 'In distant Delhi, the debate on Dara has acquired a rarefied political dimension. Was the Wadhwa Commission right in suggesting that there "is no evidence that any authority or organisation was behind the gruesome killings" of the Staines'? Is Dara a loner, a self-appointed loose cannon flaunting a Hindu label? Or is he a closet extension of the Bajrang Dal?'

Paul and Angie, the dormitory parents I stayed with at Hebron, were in Ooty when Graham and the boys

were killed, and they became close to Gladys in
the aftermath. A year after the deaths, they visited
her in Baripada. Paul did a few odd jobs on the
property—like Graham, he is a down-to-earth man
with a knack for building and repairing with local
materials. But really, Angie told me, they were there
to support Gladys.

In the months following the deaths, Gladys unwillingly
became a media superstar and the face of Christianity
in India. She told the press that she would not return
to Australia but would carry on Graham's work, that
India was her home. Newspapers and magazines—at
least, the English-language ones—rallied around her
and declared her a heroine. Liberal Hindu leader Swami
Agnivesh praised her in the *Times of India*: 'It speaks
volumes of the greatness of Gladys that even after such a
terrible trauma, she is keen to stay on and continue the
work of her husband ... It is not surprising that people
all over the country, cutting across barriers, recognised
this as the finest moment of true spirituality.'

Possibly, the image of Gladys as a widow—always
dressed in a pale sari, grieving but strong—tapped
into an Indian archetype. Indira Gandhi, the steel-
willed and hugely popular prime minister, had been a
sari-clad widow. I still saw busts and paintings of her
as I travelled around India twenty-five years after her
assassination, and now the image of Italian-born Sonia
Gandhi, widow of Indira's son Rajiv, is everywhere.

Paul and Angie didn't think Gladys was as strong and sure during that first year as she appeared in the media. 'It was hard for her,' Paul said. 'Graham had been the admin man who ran everything, and people kept coming to her with big important decisions she had to make, and she wasn't always up to it.' Despite this, Gladys's unwanted celebrity brought a lot of donations to the mission, Paul told me. The funds were used to build a hospital on the mission compound, the Graham Staines Memorial Hospital, and to bring in medical staff from around India.

Five years later, when Esther finished school and decided to study medicine in Australia, Gladys quietly returned there with her daughter. She said she needed to support Esther, as well as her elderly father, and that she would take the chance to study and update her nursing skills. After another five years, she visited India regularly, but remained based in Australia.

In about 2007 the weekend magazine in the *Australian* newspaper ran a cover article about Gladys and her life in Queensland; in my memory she wore a blue blouse that matched her eyes, and she stood in front of a cane field. She wasn't holding herself as stiffly as she did in the Indian photographs, when she wore a sari and pressed her hands together in a namaste or accepted a garland or a plaque or a book from a preacher or a government official. She was working as a nurse, the article said, and caring for her elderly father, supporting Esther in her medical studies and growing vegetables in her garden. I imagined her gardening peacefully on her own, with her hands in the soil, just like my own mother in her herb garden.

Twelve years after Graham, Philip and Timothy Staines were killed, cases relating to the deaths were still being heard in the Indian courts. Dara Singh was sentenced to death in 1999, but the High Court of Orissa overturned the ruling in 2005, commuting it to a life sentence on the grounds that Singh had not been proved to have personally caused the deaths.

Use of the death penalty is extremely uncommon in India. In 1995 a serial-killing autorickshaw driver from Chennai known as Auto Shankar was hanged, but at the time of writing there has been only one other killing by the state since then. India's death row contains the only surviving member of the terrorist gang that attacked sites around Mumbai in 2008, along with the surviving assassins of prime minister Rajiv Gandhi, and various other killers, including a few Maoists.

In 2007 India's Central Bureau of Investigation moved to have Dara Singh's death sentence reinstated, arguing that he had confessed to the killings. It took until January 2011 for the Supreme Court to reach a decision to uphold the life sentence rather than restore the death penalty.

Gladys Staines and Indian Christian groups had not asked for the death penalty. They were not out for revenge, they said. They had forgiven the killers. Life in prison was appropriate, they thought.

Less appropriate were the comments made by the judges who upheld the life sentence. Graham Staines had been behaving in an intolerant way, they implied, and so it was understandable that people had responded with intolerance of their own; the mob was trying 'to teach a lesson to Graham Staines about his religious activities', the judgement said. It also noted that 'it is undisputed that there is no justification for interfering in someone's belief by way of "use of force", provocation, conversion, incitement or upon a flawed premise that one religion is better than the other'.

Many Indian people were horrified by the judges' comments, which they interpreted to mean that Graham Staines had deserved his death, that this was the understandable result of preaching his religion. A statement against the judgement was signed by journalists, editors and private citizens across the country and was printed in the *Hindu*, which also ran a report:

> Arguing that the [judges'] remarks were 'gratuitous,' 'unconstitutional' and went against the 'freedom of faith' guaranteed by the Constitution, the signatories asked that they be expunged … The signatories said the Supreme Court and other judicial forums were secular India's last hope to preserve constitutional guarantees given to

religious minorities and other marginalised groups. Judgments such as this one and the Ayodhya verdict delivered by the Allahabad High Court were disturbing because they could be interpreted as 'supporting the bigoted point of view of right wing fundamentalists such as the Sangh Parivar.'

It is interesting that a link was made between the Staines case and the Ayodhya case—the ongoing argument over who owns the temple or mosque grounds in Ayodhya. A few months before the Dara Singh ruling, in late 2010, the Allahabad High Court ruled, somewhat unexpectedly, that the Ayodhya site be split three ways, with equal portions given to a Muslim organisation and two Hindu groups. In a move that was much easier to predict, all three groups thought they had been cheated. They all appealed the decision.

It took only a few days of protest for the Supreme Court to review its comments about Graham Staines and Dara Singh. The paragraph about Graham being taught a lesson was removed from the official record, and the court instead said that the reason not to reinstate the death penalty was simply because of the time that had elapsed since the deaths. The language about conversions was softened, a little.

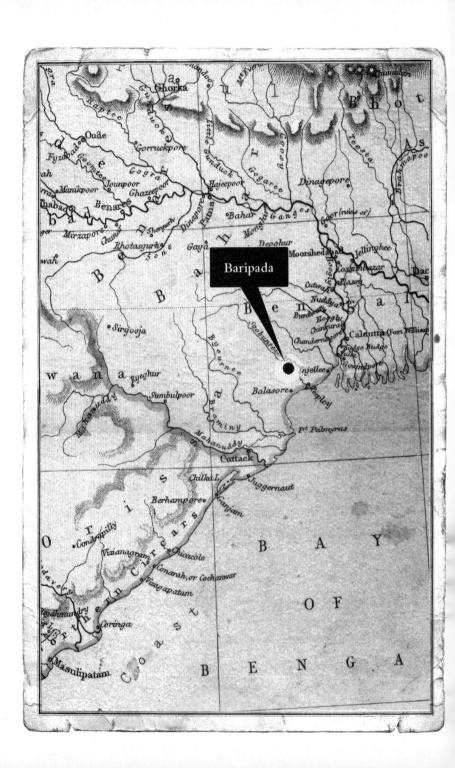

7

BARIPADA

The train from Bhubaneswar to Baripada didn't have any air-conditioning or first-class carriages. There was only one class, with wooden seats rather than berths. I had started to get used to travelling in the three-tier air-conditioned carriages, which are a step up from what we were able to afford in the 1980s, and this may be why I'd been imagining that travel in India had become cleaner and easier than it was when I was a child. Steam trains were still common then, and if you sat by an open window you ended up with specks of soot all over your skin and clothes, like tiny black freckles. This grotty old train was like the trains we used to travel in. The metal window frames were too grubby to rest my elbow on, and the simultaneously chilly and humid air that rushed through the windows left my skin clammy and my hair greasy and whipped into knots. I pulled a headscarf from my bag and wrapped it round my hair, and I looked at the women around me and felt jealous of them; they all had long, oiled hair pulled into tight plaits that seemed immune to any muss.

The train wasn't very crowded. The other passengers looked poorer, thinner and less carefully dressed than my usual fellow travellers. These people were on their way home to their villages, I guessed. Perhaps they had been doing menial jobs in the capital to earn money to take home. Even the snack sellers on the train were different: instead of carrying bags of brand-name chips and bottles of Coke, these men carried dirty baskets containing random items like boiled eggs and wrinkled pieces of fruit.

Outside, the edges of Bhubaneswar looked very poor. We rattled past encampments where raggedly dressed women stood in front of shacks, while others washed clothes in muddy patches of a creek. Dogs covered in sores scratched themselves or sat listlessly by the tracks. It was late afternoon, and the sky was grey.

When my family lived in Ooty, other teachers and missionaries used to refer to Orissa as 'the back of beyond', and missionaries working in the state were considered braver and hardier than any others. Over the years I built up a picture of a filthy, lawless place, and when I finally travelled there myself as an adult I was pleasantly surprised at how friendly the people were to foreigners and how attractive the state was. I loved the medieval temples of Bhubaneswar, the Sun Temple in Konark, the beaches of Puri, the green hills and colourful markets of the south and the overgrown wildlife sanctuaries of the north.

But today I felt as if I was, in fact, travelling to the back of beyond. As the sky grew darker I started to feel alone. For possibly the first time ever in India, I also felt unsafe. Every young man who looked at me seemed to be furtively planning some kind of attack. I imagined the train stopping in the middle of nowhere in the dark. Where would I go?

I was still rattled by my mother's stupid dream, as well as thinking about Graham's death. Most people are good people, I thought. I unzipped my bag, took out my notebook and wrote the words down. 'MOST PEOPLE ARE GOOD PEOPLE.' Statistically, the likelihood of anything happening to me was incredibly low. Even if one person wanted to hurt me, others would help me.

Once upon a time, feeling like this, I might have prayed. Even now, my first impulse when I'm frightened is to think 'Help me, Jesus.' But I don't believe that's any proof that Jesus is real, or even that deep down I still believe Jesus to be real. When I was a child it was drummed into me that I should ask Jesus for help when I was in trouble, and now I reach for it without thinking, in the same way that someone might reach for a gun they no longer carry.

Perhaps that isn't the best analogy.

I tried to breathe slowly, but I felt a tight band around my chest. I sipped water from the bottle I'd been clutching for the last couple of hours. People survive travelling alone, I thought. It's not even going to be hard. I imagined Graham arriving at a house with no electricity, and earlier missionaries faced with bullock-cart transport and furniture made of kerosene tins, and knew I was lucky. Someone was going to pick me up at the Baripada train station, after all. I imagined a smiling young man holding a homemade sign—my name written in felt-tip pen on a piece of cardboard. I would not have a panic attack. Was I already having a panic attack? I sipped water and willed myself to breathe slowly for another two hours.

At about ten in the evening the train reached Baripada, the end of the line. The same maharajah who gave land to missionaries for the leprosy mission more than a hundred years ago also paid to have the train line extended to Baripada. The station is small and was lit up brightly with fluorescent tubes. Beyond it, the town looked very dark.

The other passengers all walked out into the night, and the station became quiet. I stood on the platform looking at the car park, which was empty except for a couple of autorickshaws. One of the drivers called out to me, asking if I needed a ride, and I said, 'No, Uncle is coming,' and he shrugged and went back to talking to the other driver. 'Uncle' was a term they would understand;

it means any older man who is part of the family, or a friend of the family. It's a respectful term, coming from a younger person.

I waited for five minutes, and nobody came to pick me up. I realised that I did not have Subhankar's phone number, only an email address. I didn't know what to do except stand there, thinking '*Iyoh, iyoh*'— the Indian equivalent of 'Oh dear'. In retrospect, if nobody had come I could have just asked the auto driver to take me to a hotel, but at that moment I was frozen.

Of course, someone came. A young man ran up to me, out of breath, and asked, 'Are you Kate?' He pronounced my name naturally, rather than the usual tortured 'Ketta' or 'Kits', and I knew he must be from the Evangelical Missionary Society of Mayurbhanj, which had been founded in 1899 by another Australian called Kate.

Like Graham Staines, Kate Allenby was twenty-four years old when she first arrived in the Mayurbhanj region of Orissa. She had been born and raised in Queensland. An early photo shows a small, pretty woman wearing a high-necked, bulky dress and holding an accordion, which was no doubt considered a useful tool for teaching Christian songs to the natives.

Kate had travelled to Mayurbhanj at the invitation of the local maharajah, whose palace in Baripada is now a college where Graham Staines's friends Subhankar and Mira Ghosh both used to teach. The palace gates are still decorated with images of peacocks, the symbol of the local princes: 'Mayurbhanj' means 'home of the peacock'. The maharajah, Ram Chandra Bhanj Deo, had been influenced by his English tutor, a devout Christian, and he gave Kate free rein to travel, preach and provide health care throughout the region. She went from village to village by elephant or bullock cart, through open fields, charting her own maps, sleeping in the back of the cart at night after lighting a fire to keep tigers away. She learned Oriya and Santali, and translated the catechism into Santali.

Over the years other Australian missionaries joined Kate, and in the early 1900s the maharajah donated two pieces of land just outside Baripada to the Evangelical Missionary Society of Mayurbhanj, to be used for homes for beggars and people suffering from leprosy.

Kate Allenby died of a stroke in Baripada in 1931, aged sixty. Hundreds of locals came to take a last look at her before she was laid to rest in the same Christian cemetery where Graham, Philip and Timothy were buried in 1999. On the wall at the mission house in Baripada there's a photo of Kate taken the year before she died. She's posed in the same way as in the photo taken of her as a young woman, but in this picture her hair is grey, she's wearing a sari rather than a Victorian gown, and instead of an accordion she's holding cards with Oriya script on them. She looks like a tough old bird.

The young man who had come to pick me up smiled and said, 'I'm five minutes late.' He led me to a jeep and drove me through the town to the mission compound. We pulled up in front of the Graham Staines Memorial Hospital—the name is painted in big letters on the front of the building—and Mira and Subhankar stepped out. They were already dressed for bed; Mira was wearing a long nightie and a shawl, and Subhankar a lungi. Mira held out her arms to me and said, 'Welcome, welcome,' and hugged me enthusiastically. Subhankar was more quiet, but he smiled and welcomed me. ('He's a lovely man,' my notebook from Baripada says. 'He's calm and considered and kind, and also maybe never quite recovered—there's a sadness about him. Mira's energy is louder.')

Subhankar said goodnight and disappeared into the darkness, and Mira led me into the hospital and up the stairs to the second floor, where the nurses live. We walked past a large, empty room with the words 'Philip & Timothy Memorial Hall' painted in big red letters on the wall and into a common area with a computer, sink, gas ring and plastic chairs. A map of Australia was taped to the wall. I stopped in front of it and saw that someone had used a biro to draw an arrow pointing to Townsville, where Gladys and Esther live. Other arrows pointed to different Queensland towns, and names were written on the map. I presumed they were the names of supporters of the mission who had visited Baripada.

I was introduced to a couple of nurses, young women wearing salwar kameezes. They giggled, and one of them asked, excited, 'Do you know Aunty?' She meant Gladys.

'I met Gladys at Hebron School when I was a teacher there,' I replied. I showed them on the map how far south of Townsville I live, in Melbourne.

Mira gestured for me to sit and uncovered a plate of egg curry and chapatis that had been waiting on the table. I thanked her and was about to pick up a chapati when she sat down next to me, took my hand and launched into a long prayer, thanking God for the food and for bringing me there safely, because I was there to do the work of the Kingdom.

This was awkward.

When I had first planned the trip to India, I had emailed Gladys Staines and asked if she minded my writing about her husband and boys. I sent her a copy of my first book and explained that, while I was no longer a Christian, I was sympathetic to Christians. Gladys had replied, asking me to be careful to be factually correct, and she had contacted Mira and Subhankar to let them know I would be visiting. I had assumed that she would have warned them about my irreligiousness, but I suspected now that she hadn't even remembered; she met a lot of people, I knew, and we hadn't corresponded at any length. Mira and Subhankar probably knew me only as a Hebron School connection.

I nodded at the end of the prayer, but I didn't say 'Amen' with Mira. I thanked her for saving food for me and ate everything, including the slimy green ladyfinger chutney that always made me gag when it was served up in the Hebron dining hall. Mira showed me to my room and told me that hospital prayers were held at eight-fifteen in the morning. I was to share the bathroom down the hall with the nurses.

I lay awake knowing that I had to say something before I was asked to preach. This was going to be even harder than preparing a talk for schoolboys about the scientific method. I was trying to think of a way of explaining myself that wouldn't make me look bad to Mira and Subhankar, that would be somehow acceptable. I knew there would be a distance between us after I told them the truth. I realised how much I wanted these people to like me. I still wanted to be considered one of them; I wanted my atheism to take a form they could approve of, which I knew wasn't possible. It had been the same when I first 'came out' to my family: I knew I was removing myself from them. I had heard them speaking about former Christians over the years, not with anger but with sadness. The way they talked about them made it clear that they were no longer 'one of us'. I hated the thought of that happening to me. I wanted to be one of them without being one of them, to have it both ways.

A patch of yellow from an outside light cut through the window between the curtains, and I could see a couple of geckoes on the wall above the window, big and pale. Eventually I slept, more heavily than I'd expected to.

Mira woke me early, bringing me a cup of tea, and after I'd had a cold bucket bath I sat out at the communal table, reading a book under the map of Australia. Subhankar came upstairs to take me to prayers, and I swallowed and said I needed to say something to him.

'Of course,' he said, sitting down next to me.

I said that while I had grown up with Christian family and community and still loved them all, a couple of years ago I'd almost had a breakdown over the whole issue of my faith not being my own. I'd realised that I had just been keeping my family happy, and since then I hadn't called myself a Christian, but only a seeker. (I didn't say of what, and I did not describe myself as an atheist.) I told Subhankar that I needed to be honest with him and Mira about that, and that it wasn't appropriate for me to preach or pray in public.

Subhankar just nodded and said 'Okay,' and then he took me downstairs. He said he wanted to show me the plaques on the front of the hospital.

Outside, he pointed out the plaque that had been laid by a man called Santanu Satpathy, who had been

Graham's oldest friend in India. In the late 1950s
Satpathy, a bright teenage boy living near Baripada,
asked the Australian missionary Vera Stevens to find
him an Australian penpal, and his address made its way
to Graham. The pair turned out to have been born on
the same day in 1941, and they corresponded for eight
years before Graham sailed to Orissa and they met in
person. They remained close friends until Graham's
death. Satpathy had visited Baripada just a few days
before Graham's final drive to Manoharpur, and
Gladys had served cake to celebrate their birthdays.

Satpathy had studied engineering and worked in
other parts of India, but after Graham died he returned
to Baripada and helped to build the new hospital. I had
read about the pair and their friendship, but what I
hadn't known until now was that Satpathy had never
been persuaded by Graham's beliefs.

'He's still a Hindu; he's not yet a Christian,'
Subhankar said. 'Not yet,' he said, of an intelligent man
of nearly seventy years who had been talking to Christian
missionaries for most of his life.

And so we went to prayers. The hospital staff sang
unaccompanied songs in Oriya. I picked up recognisable
phrases: '*Jisu Rajah*' must mean 'King Jesus', I thought.
Subhankar led a Bible reading and gave some exposition
in English, which was translated into Oriya by one of
the doctors. I worried that the English was just for my
sake, but it turned out there were other visitors. After

he had prayed, Subhankar introduced the staff to me and to a Malayali family sitting behind me. They had travelled from the southern state of Kerala to visit the mission. The couple were well dressed and had three small children. The youngest girl, a toddler, wore a dress covered with sparkles and sequins. The father's greying hair had been dyed red with henna.

The doctors and nurses went to work, and the Malayali family and I were led through the leafy compound, past the whitewashed church built in 1905, and into the old mission house, where we were served breakfast. I loved the mission house, a solid old whitewashed concrete building with dark-wood doors and high wooden ceilings. The colonial architecture reminded me of the missionary guesthouse my mother managed in Ooty when we first moved to India. This is where the Staines family used to live, and where Mira and Subhankar now live when they are in Baripada. The walls of the mission house were decorated with posters of landscapes with Bible verses written underneath, calendars from various mission organisations and framed watercolours showing idealised scenes of Indian village life. Photos of the Staines family were on display, along with a lurid Photoshopped picture of Graham and the boys with flames behind them, next to a picture of the burned-out jeep in which they were killed. I didn't ask where it had come from.

I could imagine a young Australian family living here; it was easy to picture Philip and Timothy running in and out of these rooms. I was touched by little pieces of Australiana in the house: Tupperware like my grandmother's, an Australian wildflowers tea towel used as a mat for the DVD player to sit on. I thought again of my native Australian animals tablecloth and wondered whether Gladys and Esther now decorate their home in Australia with Indian memorabilia.

Breakfast was chapatis, omelettes and more ladyfingers, which we ate while introducing ourselves. Afterwards, we moved into the living room for another round of songs and prayers in Oriya with the mission's domestic staff. The Malayali man, whose name was John, was asked to 'bring a word' to the staff. He spoke at length in English—with translation from Mira—about how he had been diagnosed with high cholesterol and had needed surgery but Jesus had healed him. 'Praise God,' he said. John told us that he and his wife had received separate messages from the Holy Spirit, who had told them they were to go and work in Orissa, and now they were travelling around the state and praying about it. They were considering opening a Christian school, perhaps even here in Baripada.

It took John a long time to tell this story, with its many less than interesting diversions. One of the domestic staff—I think he was a gardener—fell asleep. I heard him snore, very softly.

John said that his wife's leading by the Holy Spirit to move to Orissa had come when she saw footage of the funeral of Graham Staines and the boys and heard the song that Gladys wrote for the funeral, 'Because He Lives'.

'Gladys didn't write that song,' Mira and I both said, almost at the same time.

'It's an old song,' Mira added.

John and his wife looked completely taken aback, as if this changed everything, as if perhaps they had misunderstood the Holy Spirit's message if the song had not been written by Gladys. John stumbled back into the thread of his story, but with less confidence than before.

Afterwards, when the staff dispersed, John approached me. 'Are you in ministry, Sister?' he asked.

Let's face it: with no makeup, a salwar kameez and a matronly figure, I looked very much like a missionary. I was just glad he hadn't called me 'Aunty'. I said that I wasn't in ministry and explained that I was researching a book about Graham Staines.

John brightened up, saying 'Aah' as if this was an excellent thing. 'What church do you attend?' he asked, and I said, 'I don't attend any church,' and he said, more clearly, 'I'm sorry, I asked which church do you attend?' and I answered again, and he looked at his wife, who was standing next to him and who I suspected spoke better English than he did, and she said something to him in Malayalam, and he looked puzzled and said 'Oh.'

I felt bad, but not bad enough to try to explain as I had done for Subhankar. 'Long story,' I said.

Later in the morning, Mira and Subhankar took the Malayali family and me in a jeep to visit Baripada's Christian cemetery and the Staines graves. I had expected the cemetery to be attached to a church, but it's just a piece of land. A wall, freshly whitewashed, has been built around it, with a locked wrought-iron gate. I had read somewhere that people had attempted to vandalise the graves, but when I asked Subhankar he said he wasn't aware of any such attempt.

The sun was bright and hot. Inside, some tall tropical trees had dropped big, crunchy leaves all over the ground. The graves are spread untidily around the block. Some are for British officers who died of cholera in the nineteenth century, while Kate Allenby's simple cross has only her name and the dates 1871–1931. Newer stones have been laid for local Christians. Although the Bible doesn't mandate any particular form of disposing of the bodies of believers, Indian Christians copy the traditions of foreign missionaries rather than burning their dead. It's a way to differentiate themselves from Hindus.

And then there was the monument to Graham, Philip and Timothy. Their names and dates of birth are there, and underneath are the words 'Martyred for Christ on 23rd January 1999 at Manoharpur village while proclaiming God's love.' English and Oriya text then tells Graham's story: 'Graham came from Australia to Mayurbhanj in 1965. He served leprosy people, shared God's love among Oriya, Santhali & Ho people, spoke their language fluently and proclaimed the good news of God's Kingdom. He was loved by all, and his heart was in Mayurbhanj.'

He wasn't loved by everyone, I thought. He wasn't loved by the trolls online who write comments like 'Long live Dara Singh for roasting Graham "Crispy" Staines and his bitch kids' under YouTube clips about him.

I cried, just a little. If I was a Christian they would have been uncomplicated tears, but I don't know what made me sadder: the deaths, or the fact that I don't believe this good man and his sweet sons are with Jesus. They are just gone, like thousands of Indian Christians—and Muslims, and Hindus, for that matter—who have died useless deaths because of religion, or the pretence of religion.

I felt guilty because I wasn't crying for all of them, or trying to tell all their stories. Why was I writing about an Australian's death, and not about the killing of a priest from Kerala or the attacks on Adivasi Christians? I didn't have a good answer, other than that I have a kind of shared history with Graham and his boys, and I understand what their lives must have been like.

They were my people.

I'd come to India to see the graves for myself because of the sadness I had felt every time I had thought of them for ten years. But I didn't have any revelation once I was there. Nothing was resolved.

I liked the angels on the memorial stone. I was surprised to see them: evangelical Christians tend to be minimalist about decoration, but there's something almost Victorian about these angels; one of them holds a rose and the other is blowing a trumpet. The names of Gladys and Esther are written underneath the angels, as if these are in fact pictures of Gladys and Esther. In an ABC radio interview in Australia in 2003, Gladys said that 'Timothy used to love roses, so on Timothy's grave we have actually got an angel holding a rose. He used to make up his own little songs and he used to sing "When we get to heaven we will all be given a rose."'

I thought I should take a photo of the memorial, and when John saw me with my camera he posed his family behind it, all of them carefully looking somber, and he called Mira and Subhankar over to stand with them.

'We should go to the leprosy centre now,' Mira said, after I took a photo, and we all walked back to the jeep.

While we drove, Mira talked about the practical difficulties of administering the mission in the aftermath of Graham's death. Then she said, unexpectedly, that Subhankar had become very depressed after the loss of his friend. 'For months he could do almost nothing,' she said.

I turned to look at Subhankar, who was looking at the floor of the jeep.

'Many people prayed for him. Gladys prayed for him,' Mira added. He did his work, she said, but the rest of the time he just sat with his elbows on the table and his head in his hands. She showed us, putting her elbows on her knees and her hands over her face.

Subhankar nodded.

I would have liked to reach out and put a hand on his hand, but I knew it wouldn't be appropriate.

The leprosy treatment centre and the nearby rehabilitation home are big leafy properties outside the town, with simple stone and concrete buildings busy with people who gave us wide smiles and folded their hands to say 'Namaste' but kept working. At the rehabilitation home, women were sweeping up piles of dry leaves and using them to stoke a fire. They were cooking a communal meal in a huge blackened dekshi that my father would have referred to as a pot big enough for cannibals to cook a missionary in. It didn't seem like a funny joke in this context. A couple of chickens ran squawking past us, almost knocking over the Malayali toddler.

I noticed that some of the people who greeted us had stubby hands, with missing or shortened fingers. I tried not to look, but Mira pointed out the hands, as well as people's feet, explaining that these patients had come to the centre for treatment when their leprosy was advanced. The younger residents of the home had fewer physical problems because they had received more modern treatment and had been treated earlier.

We walked into a whitewashed chapel with a plaque outside that read 'To the glory of God—the gift from the mission to the lepers in the east—1907.' I took a photo of it. I liked the rather un-PC use of 'leper', a word I hadn't heard used unmetaphorically since Sunday School. 'The lepers.' It was a bit like 'the gays' or 'the cripples'. I'd heard a lot about cripples in Sunday School too, as Jesus was always healing them, but not so much about gays. I remembered the term used on Graham's gravestone—'leprosy people'.

'People always talk about how Christians are just trying to make conversions, but we did a survey recently and only nine of the sixty-six people who live here are Christians,' Subhankar said. He admitted that most of the former leprosy patients, who still lived at the home, attended services in the chapel, but said that this was only out of politeness to the people who had helped them.

While we were talking a man came to the chapel door and waved at Subhankar.

'Come in, come in,' Subhankar said, and he ushered the man over. He was elderly, wearing shorts and an old shirt. 'This is Josia,' Subhankar told me, as if I should know who the famous Josia was, and in fact I did: this was the Josia whose photo, shown at Graham Staines's church in Queensland in the early 1960s, had inspired Graham to move to India.

Josia led us over to another 'leprosy person', a man who was sitting outside in the sun with sheets of rubber and tools around him, making special shoes for residents of the home who had problems with their feet. This is one of the most common afflictions, Subhankar said. 'He sells them rather than giving them away, but still at a loss,' he told me. 'It's important to make people value their shoes.'

We were shown piles of grass that the residents weave into mats and baskets that are sold in Baripada's market. In the workshop, hanging on the wall, was another piece of grass work, but this was decorative: a stylised circle or wheel of fire, like the fire that Shiva dances within as Nataraj in paintings and statues, only this one was empty.

The last stop on our tour was even further out of town. After the Graham Staines Memorial Hospital was finished, donations to the mission were funnelled into building a home to which boys from remote villages are sent so they can attend school in Baripada. It is called the Philip and Timothy Memorial Hostel, and it is, by Western standards at least, extremely basic. The twenty-three boys sleep on mats on the concrete floor in a couple of very simple rooms, with just one carer. In the grounds is a well that the boys pump themselves for all cleaning and drinking water, and a vegetable patch has been planted and is tended by the boys. Lights have recently been installed after solar panels were donated to the hostel. The boys have one cotton shirt and one pair of shorts each, and they have to look after them carefully.

The Malayali boy, dressed in a silk kurta and long pants, looked around with interest, while the boys living in the hostel stood silently by the well, and then he whispered to his father.

'Can he have a drink?' John asked.

Subhankar spoke in Oriya to one of the boys, who ran to fetch a cup. He pumped water from the well and handed it to the Malayali boy in a deferential way— carefully, with both hands, not looking him in the face.

The whole scene reminded me vividly of the passage in *Jane Eyre* when the minister who runs Jane's very poor orphanage brings in his silk-clad, ringleted nieces to tour the premises. The rich girls gawk at the quiet orphans, who have just been given a lecture about the evils of curled hair and the importance of simplicity in dress.

I'm not saying it was a fair comparison for me to make.

When I was working at Hebron School in 1997, one of my responsibilities was to check that the junior school students had washed their hands before they filed into the dining hall for lunch. Here, at the Philip and Timothy home for boys, I had a sudden memory of Philip Staines smiling and holding up his hands as close to my face at he could get them, enthusiastically waving them to show me how clean they were.

As we walked back to the jeep we picked up some tamarind pods that had fallen from a tree. Subhankar split a pod open, and the Malayali children and I chewed on the sour pulp, spitting out shiny seeds as we walked.

In addition to being too cold to sustain monkeys, Ooty is also too cold for tropical trees like tamarinds, but every time we travelled on the plains when I was a child I took the chance to chew on tamarind straight from the tree. My mouth still fills with saliva just thinking about it. Tamarind always reminds me of the holiday my family spent with the Bible translators Ray and Elisabeth Valentine. The main food in their village was ragi, a porridge that was used for plugging holes in walls as well as for eating. I hated ragi and tried to subsist on tamarind instead. The Valentine children showed us how to climb the trees, and we braved the monkeys to get to the sour pods. My stomach never thanked me.

On the way home we drove past the Baripada jail. It is an attractive colonial redbrick building, and the sign for it has peacocks painted on it. Later, I saw similar peacocks on a sign outside a children's park.

'Dara Singh is still kept there,' Mira said, pointing at the jail.

I was shocked that Graham's killer was so close by. I had imagined him having been spirited off to Delhi, far away from this community.

Subhankar was quiet.

Back at the mission house we ate lunch, rice and vegetable curry, with our hands. I told Mira and Subhankar that when I had travelled in India five years earlier, almost everyone I met had wanted to talk about the Staines case, especially when I told them I was Australian. But this time, I said, people wanted to talk about the cricket.

That sounded right, Mira said. People had forgotten, and younger people had never heard of the case.

We moved on to other topics. The idea that the government was corrupt was something that everyone seemed to agree with. I told Mira and Subhankar that I had heard that the chief minister of Orissa couldn't even speak Oriya, and they laughed and said yes, that was true.

'His father was a common man and people loved him, but the son has no idea,' Subhankar said. 'He hasn't once sat down on someone's veranda and spoken with them ... and yet they accuse Graham who spoke Oriya and Santali and Ho of not being an Indian.'

Surrounded by Indian people, my accent must have been changing even further. The housekeeper, bringing us fresh tea, told me I had a nice clear accent and was easy to understand. I said that I had the same accent as Esther Staines: Australian with a hint of both Indian and 'Hebron', the transatlantic accent of our international school. The housekeeper said how much she missed Gladys and Esther and reminded me that they spoke Oriya fluently. 'They speak it together at home,' she said.

'They sing Oriya and Santali songs together.' I liked the picture of the two blondes in a Queensland home, singing together, as they had done in the cemetery.

The next morning at prayers, Subhankar read a few Bible passages about trees and fruitfulness, including King David's words from Psalm 1:

Blessed is the one who does not walk in step with the wicked or stand in the way that sinners take or sit in the company of mockers, but whose delight is in the law of the Lord, and who meditates on His law day and night. That person is like a tree planted by streams of water, which yields its fruit in season and whose leaf does not wither—whatever they do prospers.

Then he read from Jeremiah 17: 'But blessed is the one who trusts in the Lord, whose confidence is in him. They will be like a tree planted by the water that sends out its roots by the stream. It does not fear when heat comes; its leaves are always green. It has no worries in a year of drought and never fails to bear fruit.' He finished with the words of Jesus from John 15:

I am the vine; you are the branches. If you remain in me and I in you, you will bear much fruit; apart from me you can do nothing. If you do not remain in me, you are like a branch that is thrown away and withers; such branches are picked up, thrown into the fire and burned. If you remain in me and my words remain in you, ask whatever you wish, and it will be done for you. This is to my Father's glory, that you bear much fruit, showing yourselves to be my disciples.

Subhankar smiled before he prayed. I hadn't seen him look so animated before. He was a botanist; this imagery was close to his heart.

It had been years since I had been to church, but this kind of talk still felt very familiar to me: I had heard many Christian teachers who knew the Bible well take a theme or image and string together every scriptural reference to it. I could once have done it myself, easily enough. I probably still could.

I remembered a song we had sung at church and in school assemblies. All the children at Hebron had to sing Christian hymns, no matter what their religious background.

I've got roots growing down to the water,
I've got leaves growing up to the sunshine
And the fruit that I bear is a sign of life in me.
I am shade from the hot summer sundown,
I am nest for the birds of the heaven,
I'm becoming what the Lord of trees has meant
me to be.

At breakfast with Mira, Subhankar and the Malayalis, I asked Subhankar how things had changed for the mission since Graham's death.

'Leadership is the issue now,' he said. He was talking about spiritual leadership among local Christians. 'Graham made good leaders, but as these people get educated, they leave.' He said that it was important that local Christians didn't look to outsiders to guide them or care for them. 'There's growth under local leadership; we want to be just a catalyst,' he added.

Subhankar said he had noticed a trend for Christians to marry outside their tribal group, which he thought was a good thing, as it broke down traditional enmities between them. One of the nurses at the hospital was a local Adivasi woman—he used the word 'tribal'—and he hoped more tribals would seek medical training. I noticed that when Subhankar spoke about the welfare of Adivasi Christians, he switched easily between talking about their physical and their spiritual health.

I wanted to ask Subhankar about the night that Graham, Timothy and Philip died, but I couldn't find the words. I thought about Mira's description of him—silent, head in his hands—and I didn't want to hurt him further by reminding him of that night. He had already described the events to the authors of *Burnt Alive*, explaining that he and Gilbert Venz had been sleeping in a hut and had been woken by shouts and screams. Their door had been barred, but he had seen, through the window, people with burning torches breaking the windows of the jeep. 'Then suddenly I saw the jeep in flames,' he was quoted as saying. 'I knew my dear friends would be turned into ashes.'

John didn't want to let go of Subhankar's story. 'So you were there, that very night?' he asked. 'What did you see?'

I had turned to talk with Mira, but I tried to listen as Subhankar spoke softly, telling the story again. He said that from his window all he could see were the crowds and the torches and the jeep being smashed. But just for a moment, he said, he saw something pale inside the jeep. It was Philip's blond head. 'It was Philip. I saw him.' Subhankar's eyes were shiny, but they didn't spill.

That moment felt like a punch in the gut. For years I had thought about that night, the flames and the noise, but I had looked away at the last moment. Subhankar had forced me to hold my gaze.

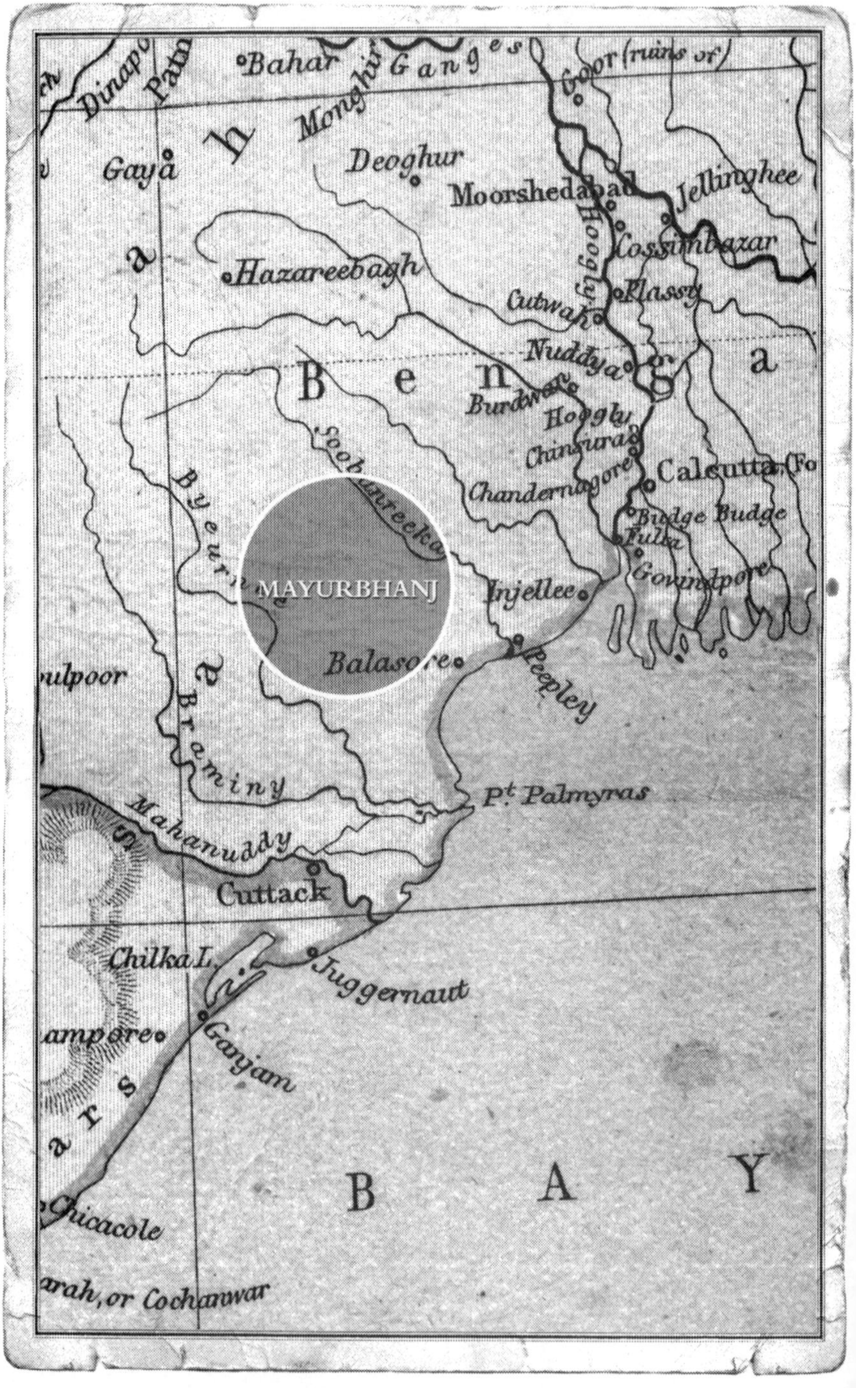
MAYURBHANJ
Bahar
Ganges
Monghir
Goor (ruins of)
Dinapore
Gaya
Deoghur
Moorshedabad
Jellinghee
Cossimbazar
Hazareebagh
Plassy
Cutwah
Nuddya
Bengal
Burdwan
Hoogly
Chinsura
Calcutta
Chandernagore
Budge Budge
Fulta
Soobanreeka
Byeturnee
Injellee
Govindpore
Balasore
Peepley
Braminy
Pt. Palmyras
Mahanuddy
Cuttack
Chilka L.
Juggernaut
Ganjam
BAY
Chicacole

8

GRAHAM STAINES

'I'm a bit worried about Gladys: she seems to be in shock,' my mother said to me on the phone the night we learned of Graham Staines's death. She had watched all the television news reports. My mother had never met the Staineses, but she spoke about them as if they were family.

I told her that Gladys wasn't necessarily in shock, but that she might just have some experience in controlling her emotions. And I told my mother about the day I had met Gladys Staines.

In 1997, to kick off my year of backpacking, I flew first to India. I'd offered to help out at Hebron for a couple of months, teaching English and music and assisting the dormitory parents who looked after the girls in classes five and six. My main job was to put the girls to bed at night with a Bible reading, a prayer and hugs, turn the lights off, then go back in and threaten them if they made any noise. Then I needed to stay in my room in case anyone wanted to come in and cry about missing their parents and be prayed with and hugged some more and sent back to bed. The girls were all ten or eleven years old. One of them was Esther Staines.

I arrived at Hebron the day before the school term started, but a mix-up with the airline meant that my bags had been left in Chennai, an overnight train journey from Coimbatore, down the hill from Ooty, and I had to go back to collect them in person. The school arranged for me to travel to the train station in Coimbatore with a group of mothers who had dropped off their children and were returning to their medical clinics, agriculture programs and orphanages across India. The women were all white, from Britain, Australia and New Zealand, and they mostly wore a salwar kameez, which was generally considered a much easier outfit for a Western woman to wear than the more complicated sari, which was more commonly worn in the south.

I took a seat next to Gladys Staines in the school bus while we waited for the driver. She wore a sari. She sat by the window talking to her son Philip, who stood outside looking up at her. He must have been seven years old, and he turned out to be, in all honesty and regardless of what went on to happen, one of the sweetest natured children I have ever met. He was crying, just a little, and Gladys was telling him that they would write to each other, that they would see each other soon, and that until then he had to be brave. She was sure he could be. She spoke kindly but briskly, with no discernible sadness.

The driver arrived and the bus took off down the driveway, and Philip wiped his eyes and ran after us for a little while, waving and smiling. Gladys waved and smiled back until we rounded a corner and he was gone. And then Gladys turned her face away from everyone, discreetly, and cried, silently, for a little while.

A week after Graham Staines and his boys died, I attended a memorial service for them that was organised by the Evangelical Alliance, a group of churches and mission organisations in Melbourne. I sang familiar old-fashioned hymns with the rest of the former missionaries and missionary supporters, and imagined that I was closer to God, and my people, than I had ever been. In fact, I left within a few weeks.

By this stage, in Melbourne, radio hosts were already advertising call-ins where listeners could agree with academics who suggested that Graham Staines had been guilty of cultural imperialism and had deserved what he got. This was just one of several opinions about why he was murdered; there was even speculation online that he had been working for the CIA and had been killed when his cover was blown. After his death, Graham was also accused of hating people of other faiths, and of either forcing or luring people into Christianity.

While I was at Hebron at the beginning of this trip, I watched a copy of an Australian television documentary about the Staines case. More than anything, I was struck by the home-video clips of Graham and his family at the mission compound and leprosy home in Baripada, filmed sometime in the mid-1990s by Graham's brother Don, who was visiting from Australia. Graham had the look of a quintessential Queensland bloke; you could mistake him for the accountant he would have become if he'd stayed in his clerk's job in Beaudesert instead of resigning to go to Bible college and the mission field. He wore a neat shirt, with pens and a glasses case in the pocket, and walk shorts with long socks.

In the videos Graham showed his brother around the leprosy home, introducing him to the people with leprosy who lived and worked there, pointing out their various deformities and discussing their histories in front of them, clinically and without sentimentality. It wasn't clear whether the patients understood what he was saying. The idea of visitors touring the home to see patients like animals in a zoo made me uncomfortable, but I have seen it many times in hospitals and orphanages in India, and not just from foreigners and missionaries.

The documentary also showed parts of the memorial service held for Graham, Philip and Timothy by their family and friends in Beaudesert. Graham's brothers, Don and John, sang in close harmony a hymn about holding on in the face of a storm.

In times like these you need a Saviour,
In times like these you need an anchor;
Be very sure, be very sure
Your anchor holds and grips the Solid Rock!
In times like these you need the Bible,
In times like these O be not idle;
Be very sure, be very sure
Your anchor holds and grips the Solid Rock!

Don and John reminded me of my mother's extended family, a Brethren clan in which men with little formal education preach and sing confidently in public settings. I thought of my uncles, Martin and Mervyn, singing 'I'll Wish I Had Given Him More' at my grandfather's eightieth birthday party.

Don spoke about martyrdom as if it was a positive thing. 'The blood of the martyrs is the seed of the church,' he quoted. I winced at the word 'martyr', imagining how it would come across to most viewers, who would think of young Muslim terrorists with explosives strapped to their bodies. The difference was that Graham didn't set out to be a martyr, I thought.

A couple of months after the deaths, a group of Indian religious leaders led by Swami Agnivesh joined together and travelled from Delhi to Baripada to meet Gladys. The documentary followed the group of Muslims, Catholics, Hindus, Sikhs and Jains on their journey. They all ate together on the train; for many of them, eating alongside someone of another religion was a huge concession and symbolically important. They stopped at railway stations along the way and gave press conferences, condemning the killings. I liked the cut of the swami's gib. He was part of a movement called Arya Samaj, a Hindu version of Christianity's liberation theology. It sounded like the opposite of Hindutva.

The travelling group called itself 'Religion for Social Justice', and the travellers talked about the importance of tolerance and suggested that really, all religions have the same goal, that the search for meaning and striving towards the infinite are not limited to any one faith, that none of us has all the answers. On almost every train trip I have taken in India I have become involved in a conversation with an intelligent, educated Hindu, a teacher or a businessman, who has voiced the same ideas.

They were lovely sentiments, but I suspected they weren't going to fly with Gladys Staines, and I was right. When the pilgrims finally reached Baripada and met Gladys, she was gracious and welcoming, but she did not seem willing to talk like them. Instead, she took the chance to share the gospel with them. 'It's because of the Lord Jesus Christ that I am here,' she said, and turned to look at the camera. I found her attitude perversely appealing.

Graham's early letters home from India (reproduced in the book *Mayurbhanj Messengers*, a history of the mission) were full of local colour, descriptions that must have sounded exotic to the family in Queensland. He described bucket baths and squat toilets, guarding the mango trees from young fruit thieves, keeping weevils out of the food and storing drinking water 'in big earthenware pots as in Bible pictures'. He bought bananas and pawpaws at the market and said that 'goat meat is also very nice. You wait while it is killed.' When I read this, I couldn't help remembering that he was only twenty-four when he wrote it and might have enjoyed shocking his mother, just a little.

His letters also included descriptions of Hindu and Adivasi holidays and festivals at which he and the other Christians often took the chance to join the festivities by handing out Christian literature and 'giving a Christian witness'. It doesn't sound like terribly good manners to me, intruding on someone else's holiday like that, but Graham was convinced that these celebrations were of the devil.

It rends one's heart to see hundreds of men, women, boys and girls pouring past the house here in the past few days ... It is the big worship holiday when the idol Durga is worshipped. They spend the whole night watching dances of the myths ... There is so much we see each day that reminds us we are in the devil's territory and he is determined not to yield one inch of it if possible.

There is no reason to believe that Graham's way of looking at these things changed over the years, despite his becoming fluent in the local dialects and making close friendships with many Indians of faiths different from his own. He absolutely believed that all religious and animistic belief apart from Christianity oppressed and hurt people, and that only genuine belief in salvation through Jesus Christ could save them in this world and the next. He learned much more about Indian customs, but he continued to see Hinduism as ultimately anti-Christian and dangerous.

In 1977, in an Australian Christian newspaper called *New Life*—the first place I ever heard of Graham, who was quoted regularly in its pages—he wrote: 'The sight of children with burn marks upon their temples and on their stomachs because the witch doctor has sought to free them from evil spirits with red hot irons only quickens the missionary's resolve to bring light to these people.' When I first read this statement, I didn't know where to start in thinking what was wrong with it. Later, I realised that of course the practices he was describing were horrible, but they were hardly central tenets of Hinduism. Education and health care seem to be what were needed, rather than a change of religion. And as far as harming people in the name of freeing them from evil spirits—well, historically, Christianity isn't entirely free of guilt.

In January 1993, Joan Vollmer, the middle-aged mentally ill wife of a pig farmer called Ralph who lived a few hundred kilometres north of Melbourne, died after being forcibly restrained in a hot shed during a supposed exorcism ceremony carried out by her husband and some other Christians who believed her symptoms were caused by evil spirits. After Joan's husband was released on bail, he spoke to the media, explaining that she would rise from the dead at her funeral service as a witness to the power of Jesus. Ralph wore a blue singlet and a terry-towelling sunhat and spoke in a slow drawl, like a Queenslander.

The good, reasonable Christians around me shook their heads and *tsk*ed while they watched Ralph Vollmer being interviewed on the television. But they didn't think something evil had been done; they thought that the people involved in Joan's death had been unwise, or uneducated, or badly informed, and they felt very sorry for them. They thought the whole affair was sad, not to mention that it showed Christians in a bad light to the rest of the world.

In the *New Life* article, Graham had gone on to say that 'among the Hindus, human sacrifice is still practiced. It is forbidden by the Government of course, but there is no doubt it takes place. There was a dam being built about 80 km from our Mission house. The people believe that if there is human sacrifice the dam won't break. So they kidnap somebody and bury him in the concrete.' I can't tell you that this has never happened. But again, it's not a specifically Hindu command or tradition. In all the years I lived in India I heard this story time and time again from missionaries, but it was always repeated by someone who had heard it from someone else, a supposedly trusted source. It seems to be the missionary equivalent of the urban myth.

Ultimately, though, while Graham believed that all religions outside Christianity were wrong, he saw their followers simply as lost. He wanted the best for people, and he believed completely that faith in Jesus was the only way. This makes perfect sense if you grew up evangelical, as I did. But later I realised that most religious believers of most faiths don't see things that way. For Hindus, in particular, the idea of proselytism is so alien that there's an assumption that the proselytiser must have some secret, underhand purpose, some kind of material gain to be had from making converts.

Why do Christian missionaries perform charitable works? It's not just because it's the right thing to do, or because they love people so much, and it's not simply a matter of following Jesus' commands to care for the needy. Growing up, I heard a lot of talk about works as an expression of faith, of being Jesus to the suffering, but in the end it seems to come down to something that is almost a trick, even for missionaries who don't actively proselytise: you care for the sick, you run orphanages, you distribute food to the hungry and you give medicine to lepers, and when anyone asks why you do it you can then point them to Jesus and the Bible, in the hope that they will become a Christian because of your example.

Graham Staines did everything he did because he wanted people to become what he thought of as genuine Christians. He believed that their souls, not their bodies, needed to be saved. He didn't want to buy their faith, as many people have suggested. He didn't offer inducements or withhold help from people unless they converted, and there's no doubt he genuinely cared for people. But everything he did was with the aim of giving people the chance to find out about Jesus. Ultimately, for him, that was all that mattered.

Graham wrote home about a young Indian man he had met who was being baptised (by another mission group) because he had simply decided that 'Christianity had more points for it than Hinduism.' The fact that the man didn't describe his conversion in traditional evangelical terms distressed Graham. 'I tried to explain salvation to him but it is hard to get through to them in English. It is tragic to realise there are those here who will turn "Christians" out like sausages and baptise anyone who asks for it. This is a constant problem here.'

During my visit to Baripada I told Subhankar Ghosh that I had heard many complaints about Adivasis and low-caste Hindus being enticed to convert to Christianity, sometimes en masse, without really understanding what they were doing, and that Christians were 'in the numbers game'.

Subhankar paused before he replied.

'With some other missions, donors want reports with numbers of conversions,' he said eventually. 'But Graham didn't do this.'

So Subhankar also believed that dodgy conversions were taking place in Orissa? I was surprised.

'Oh yes, in many places these things happen,' he said. 'We can't say if it's genuine. Graham didn't baptise many people at all; he wanted to be sure that people were serious and understood it. People loved him a lot because of his approach. He was humble; he never pushed people.'

It is clear that this was indeed Graham's approach. He did not want anyone to call themselves a Christian unless they truly believed and understood what they were getting themselves into.

Subhankar also told me that Graham had been a member of Baripada's Rotary club, and that when he went to meetings he was never late. It seemed like a small thing to note, but for him it was an example of Graham's humility, that he never kept people waiting, unlike some men who consider themselves important and often arrive at appointments late, as if to prove that their time is more valuable than anyone else's. I like to think that if Graham had had an appointment with a leprosy person he would have been on time for that too.

More than anything, Graham appears to have been a skilled administrator. 'Everything was always accounted for,' Subhankar said. 'The books were meticulously kept.'

Even though an emotional response to a photo initially led Graham to Orissa, it was common sense and down-to-earth use of his skills that kept him going. He was a practical man who had committed himself to something, given his whole heart to it, and was following through the best way he knew how.

Towards the end of my trip I browsed the bookshelf at a hotel where travellers had swapped their old paperbacks over the years. Shelves like this always contain works by Indian authors writing in English, as well as the requisite copy of Herman Hesse's *Siddhartha* in German or Dutch. More recently, I'd been finding copies of Elizabeth Gilbert's *Eat, Pray, Love*—presumably left behind by travellers who had wanted to emulate the 'Pray' section of the book—about an American woman finding her spiritual side in India. I thought the book sounded awful.

To be fair, I hadn't actually read it. But the idea of a privileged white writer looking to Indians as spiritually advanced people who would help her on her journey struck me as a particularly patronising form of colonialism. As critic Sandip Roy wrote, 'I couldn't help wondering, where do those people in Indonesia and

India go away to when they lose their passion, spark and faith? I don't think they come to Manhattan.'

Whenever I hear about people finding themselves by travelling in India I laugh and think about the British sketch show *Goodness Gracious Me,* a parody showing young Indian backpackers taking trains around Britain in order to find themselves and have a spiritual awakening. 'I've become C of E,' the young Hindu man says condescendingly. 'I know what you're thinking, but it's more than a religion; it's a way of life.'

As I looked at the hotel's copy of *Eat, Pray, Love* on the shelf, I had a horrible thought. I was a white writer going on a journey through India. Was I just as bad as Elizabeth Gilbert and all the condescending seekers before her? I hadn't come in search of myself—I think I know by now who I am, thank you—or for any kind of religious awakening, but in some ways I was still searching.

I think, in the end, I simply wanted to be assured that Graham Staines was a good man. Even more, I wanted to know that the missionaries like him whom I had grown up around—my people—were good people who had done worthwhile things, even if I disagreed with their reasons. I wanted to continue to approve of them just as strongly as I wanted them to continue to approve of me. I didn't want to feel ashamed of them.

And when I thought of it like that, I had the closest thing to an epiphany I was going to manage on this journey, and it should have been obvious all along. I realised that my people weren't any better or worse than anyone else I had met along the way, in India or in Australia. Some of them were smart and some were kind, and the best of them were both. Graham was one of the good guys, I still believed. But some of them had been bigots. Some of them had been child molesters. Some of them would say Christianity had given them a way to be better people; others had used it as an excuse to behave badly. But, really, Christianity had given most of them a way to be the kinds of people they already were.

I didn't have to approve of them all. And, more importantly, I was going to have to man up and stop caring whether or not they approved of me. In a sense they would always be my people because of our shared history, but I really had to pull up some emotional stumps and move on.

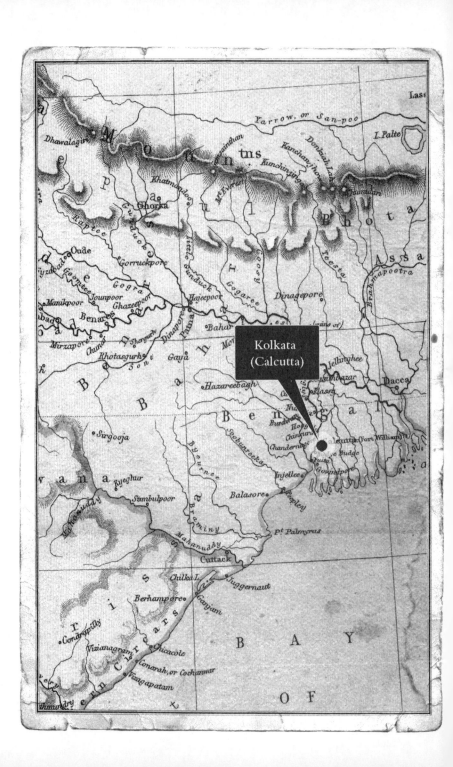

9

KOLKATA

I had planned to catch a local bus from Baripada to Kolkata. I'm not saying I thought it would be a fun few hours on the bus, but I knew there were no direct trains to Kolkata and I had assumed that regular buses would run north from Baripada to the big city. But Subhankar talked me out of my plan. He was sending the Malayali family in a jeep to a nearby town that had direct train links to the north, he said, so I should buy a ticket online and go with them. The India Rail website told me the train was full and I could buy only a waitlisted ticket online, which put me in a queue for any cancelled tickets, but Subhankar told me not to worry. He said I should just get on board and show the printout of the waitlisted ticket to the conductor, who would find me a seat. 'It's not a busy train,' he said.

I tried not to think about the large warnings on the printout of the ticket that said travelling on a waitlisted ticket was illegal and would subject the holder to fines and possible imprisonment.

When we reached the station I found my platform and squeezed onto a very crowded carriage. I stood around the doorway with some friendly young men. They asked where I was from. When I told them, one of them said, 'Oh hey, cricket! Ricky Ponting is the man!'

I told the young men I had a waitlisted ticket but had been promised I could work something out with the conductor.

The men raised their eyebrows, and one of them said, 'Maybe it will be okay because you're a foreigner, but there's no spare seats today.'

The train rolled out of the station.

The conductor turned out to be furious, or at least he was acting that way. 'No, this is illegal, madam!' he said.

'But sir, Uncle was telling me this is what I should do,' I said, trying to shift blame, like I always do.

The conductor took out his pen and underlined the warnings on my ticket so hard that it ripped the paper. He told me to stay where I was, and he marched away.

The young men didn't say anything, and they didn't look at me while I tried not to blub. I imagined I would be ordered off the train at the next station, which would no doubt be a random tiny northern Orissa town, possibly full of armed Maoists, from which I might never be able to escape.

An hour passed before the conductor returned, in which I had plenty of time to reflect on the bad thing I had done. He gestured for me to follow him down the carriage and into what looked like a baggage storage area, and he told me to sit down on a nondescript sack of something hard. He looked at me and I looked down at the floor. It was exactly like being in the principal's office.

The conductor told me again that what I had done was illegal and unacceptable. I would have to pay a big fine, he said, and I would be put off the train.

I said I understood and I was sorry.

He let his words sink in for a few moments, and then he explained what was actually going to happen. I would pay him for my ticket—the exact amount it was worth—and then he would take me to the air-conditioned carriage, where I would sit in the one free seat—his own seat. He would stay on his feet. When we reached Kolkata he would come and find me, and I would walk all the way through the station with him so that if anyone asked to see my ticket he could explain the situation.

I didn't dare to smile. 'Thank you, sir, thank you,' I said.

The conductor didn't smile either. 'Come, come,' he said, and he led me to his seat.

I thought I might vomit with relief. I sat down, looked out of the window at dusk falling over West Bengal and breathed deeply. Anyone who lives in India will laugh when I say that it didn't occur to me for days that the conductor might have been expecting a bribe, or that perhaps I should have offered one.

I spent the first day in Kolkata like an invalid, lying under the fan in my hotel room, half watching old episodes of *Friends* and *Seinfeld* on Star World, ordering cheese sandwiches and lemon drinks from room service. A few days of talking politely and fitting in with other people's timetables seemed to have wrecked me. My stomach hurt. Maybe it was the tamarind. Maybe it was *Friends*.

Early the next morning I was woken by loud music outside on the street, and a newspaper was pushed under my door. The editorial in the Kolkata edition of the *Hindu* roundly condemned the violence against Christians in Orissa, and the letters page was full of similar sentiments. I hadn't seen anything like this in the Orissa newspapers.

India's major English-language newspapers have a history of fighting communalism and tend to be supportive of Christians. When Graham Staines and his boys were killed, the *Times of India* ran a series of opinion pieces wholeheartedly condemning the direction in which Hindu nationalism was travelling. 'This country is sick and tired of the violence, injustice, oppression and fraud practiced in the name of religion,' Swami Agnivesh had written. 'The spiritual destiny of India will be fulfilled only when we realise that God is not an idol of our vested interests, but a cry of truth and justice breaking out of a heart of sacrificial love.' In the same newspaper, journalist Irene Heredi had argued that Christians had become 'a soft target—conforming, amiable, law-abiding, accustomed to protection and patronage, while right-wing extremists are intent on fast-forwarding the pages of history and mythology in a spirit of retribution, in order to establish a monocultural majoritarian state'.

I took the paper downstairs to the bar with me and ordered a chai and omelette, which I scoffed down quickly so I could walk up to the bus stand before the sun got too hot. When I arrived I wandered about, narrowly avoiding being squashed by a few buses and saying 'Belur Math?' to every bus conductor I saw until eventually I was waved onto the right bus. I knew I was nearing my destination when I noticed the 'Sri Vivekananda Pharmacy' among the tatty shops along the route. The sign showed a picture of my favourite handsome deceased wandering monk.

My destination for the day was a building that sounded, frankly, as if it was going to be a bit cheesy. It was conceived by Swami Vivekananda but wasn't completed until 1935, more than thirty years after his death. In keeping with the swami's belief in the truth of all religions, the temple was envisioned as a combination of Hindu, Muslim and Christian architecture and symbols, a monument to the faiths of India.

The Belur Math was built at the centre of the headquarters of the Ramakrishna Mission, an order founded by Vivekananda and named for his guru, the Paramahamsa, or Great Swami, Ramakrishna. Information boards at the gates of the grounds showed a picture of Ramakrishna and his wife, Sarada, sitting cross-legged together, and I had a happy moment of recognition: so that's who that was. I had seen posters and stylised paintings of the pair all over India, especially in West Bengal, and I had remembered the man because he had a big gap between his teeth. I'd known the pictures must have religious significance, but I had never worked out who the couple were.

Ramakrishna was a celibate monk, a sannyasi, when he was forced by his family to marry, and the marriage is said never to have been consummated. He saw his wife as the manifestation of the goddess, and he and his followers referred to her as the Holy Mother.

The Ramakrishna mission, as far as I could tell, is far removed in outlook from Hindu nationalism. Its aim is to do good deeds for the poor in the name of Hinduism. In the aftermath of Graham Staines's death, more than one commentator drew parallels between the work of Ramakrishna missionaries and Christians like Graham. Congress Party politician Mani Shankar Aiyar spelled it out in the national *Sunday* magazine:

....

The Ramakrishna Mission runs schools, dispensaries and hospitals ... They do their work in the name of their God ... And they receive into their fold those who wish to follow their way of life.

Graham Staines did exactly the same ... Most of his time and energies were devoted to healing the sick, comforting those in pain, tending the dying, imparting self-respect to those marginalised by society, educating the illiterate, bringing a ray of hope into the enveloping darkness. Like the missionaries of the Ramakrishna Mission, he did his work in the name of his God. But he never said: 'Isai nabin, toh dawai nahim' (If you are not a Christian, I will not give you medicine)—the grim, terrible charge trumpeted by the Bajrang Dal and other harbingers of crime in the name of religion.

....

I handed over my shoes and camera at the entrance and walked the leafy path to the Belur Math. Across the grounds the Hooghly River was attractively hazy; on the other side of the water were coconut trees and houses and what looked like an industrial refinery, all in soft focus. Indians of all classes and ages were wandering quietly around the grounds. I spotted a few European hippies, who looked to be in their fifties or sixties, meditating.

I had imagined the temple itself would be an architectural mess; in fact, it turned out to be rather lovely. Shaped like a cathedral, it has typically Muslim and Hindu ornamentation, but it's all surprisingly coherent. Inside, the temple was cool, quiet and almost empty. A priest in a saffron robe sat in front of a garlanded statue of Ramakrishna, chanting and making gestures over brass bowls of water and flowers. A few worshippers sat on the ground, cross-legged, in silence. A couple of Japanese Buddhists gazed up at the ceiling.

I sat for a long time on the marble floor of the temple, feeling very comfortable and strangely moved. I wasn't sure quite why. This was Hinduism in a form that was palatable to Westerners, the form I thought of when I argued about it being the most tolerant of religions, in spite of Hindutva and the militant nationalists. In this atmosphere I understood what people mean when they talk about 'spirituality', a concept I don't usually like.

It would be easy to have some kind of epiphany there.

Eventually, after one of my legs went to sleep, I got up and wandered over to the museum, which is full of memorabilia relating to Ramakrishna, the Holy Mother and Vivekananda. The swami's robes, shoes and books were on display, along with pictures of his various Western admirers. Copies of letters from white women started with phrases like 'To my darling boy'. I was a bit nauseated by the image of the charismatic, celibate guru with his rich, middle-aged admirers. I've seen it at church, with older women and ministers. Before I left Australia I'd been watching DVDs of *The Sopranos*, and

I suddenly pictured Vivekananda as Father Phil, the Catholic priest who develops an intensely emotional friendship with Carmela Soprano and manipulates the mafia wives into competing for his affection. And yet, in theory, I like what Vivekananda had to say.

Vivekananda founded the Ramakrishna Mission with the aim of training Hindu missionaries. He denounced caste and meaningless ritual—caring for the poor and suffering, he said, was the only way to serve the divine. Ramakrishna had been influenced by Christian and Muslim traditions of caring for the destitute in practical ways, and he passed this on to Vivekananda.

On the way back to the hotel I stopped at an internet cafe. I never know how many security procedures I'll have to go through to get online—sometimes I'm waved straight to a computer; other places ask for a photocopy of my passport; and one joint once even demanded I place my thumb on an electronic pad so my print could be kept in their system. 'Terrorists, madam,' they told me. The young man behind the desk at this place just asked for my name and phone number and suggested I buy a Coke from his fridge.

'Sure, why not,' I said.

He asked my country, and I told him. 'Ah,' he said, handing me my drink. 'Why do you keep beating us?'

I smiled. It was the cricket again. India loves Ricky Ponting. I laughed and said, 'Because we're so good.'

The young man didn't say anything.

We looked at each other and I tried to read his expression. It was something like disgust, a look I hadn't seen very often in India.

I realised, with horror, that he was not talking about the cricket. He was talking about the attacks on Indian students that had been happening recently in Australia, and particularly in Melbourne.

'Oh, no, I thought you were talking about the cricket,' I said, stumbling over my words to explain as quickly as I could. 'Everyone talks to me about the cricket. I thought you were asking why we beat you at cricket. I'm so sorry.'

He understood what I was saying, but he unstiffened only a little. 'So why is this happening?' he asked.

I didn't have any good explanations. I said it was horrible and it brought shame to us, and I meant it. I said most Australians weren't racist, that these were just a few hooligans, though I didn't know how true this was. I suspected that the Indian media had, well, beaten up the story beyond the admittedly awful facts, but I didn't think that was an appropriate thing to say. And I realised that I was there because I was writing about a lone Australian being attacked in India, while Indians were being attacked back in my home town. I felt a bit sick.

'I was going to apply to work in Australia, but now I think it's no good for Indians there,' the young man said. 'I think I'll try for the United States instead.'

I clutched my Coke and nodded.

'Now go, go, number six computer is ready,' he said.

An Australian guy was attempting to Skype at number seven computer. His connection kept disappearing, and he swore at the screen in the creative way that Australians do better than anyone else. He saw me smile, and he laughed and asked me where I was from. We turned out to live only a couple of suburbs away from each other in Melbourne. This has happened to me surprisingly regularly over the years. He said he was missing home and had been thinking about the Preston Market, where we both shopped. 'All I want is a doughnut from the hot jam doughnut stand,' he said.

I agreed and smiled but didn't laugh, because I still felt awful about the conversation with the young man. I logged in. I wanted to let Chris and my parents know I was back from the boondocks and that I was fine.

Early the next morning, while I was washing my bras in a bucket in the bathroom, I had a phone call from my friend Jane, whose parents had been teachers at Hebron School at the same time my family lived there. We grew up together; I was closer to her than to any of my cousins in Australia. Jane had gone to university at 'home' in Britain and had worked with disadvantaged teenagers there and in the United States. Later, she had joined the missionary organisation Servants to Asia's Urban Poor, which sent her to Kolkata, where she had shared a house in the slums with two other young women and attempted to—in the words of the group's mission statement—'intentionally live with the urban poor, learning from them, building genuine relationships, participating in their lives and struggles, learning their language and their culture, and working out how Jesus' love can best be shown in their context'. This, in the language of the movement, was 'incarnational living'— mimicking the way Jesus chose to become one of us, by choosing to become 'one of them'.

Jane was still in India, and I was interested in the contrast between her life and Graham Staines's more old-fashioned missionary style. I wanted to see how she lived and the places where she worked. I had contacted her before leaving Australia, and she had replied, reminding me that since her recent marriage to a Bengali church minister she hadn't actually been living in the slums. 'We're practically the middle class now,' she wrote, adding a smiley-face emoticon. She was still involved with women's projects in the slums, however, helping to administer vocational training and craft groups, and teaching English to girls.

Jane's phone call was made from a train. She was returning from a holiday to Puri with her two former housemates, and they would pick me up in a taxi on their way through the city.

I hung up my dripping bras and went downstairs, where I sat in the empty bar and read Satyajit Ray short stories, drank masala chai and ate an omelette full of green chillies.

When I stepped outside, the family that lived on the footpath were still asleep on pieces of cardboard, under plastic sheets that had been rigged up to the street lights. Stray dogs slept on the road, curled up around each other. The Holi festival had recently been celebrated, in which people threw bright-coloured powders at each other in the street, and the dogs must have got in the way; their coats were still stained with pink and purple patches. The taxi wallahs were washing their cars with water that was gushing from a burst pipe. A man wearing a suit prayed in front of a Durga shrine set up under a tree. We were right in the centre of town, but a man was leading a herd of goats along the road.

When the taxi pulled up, Jane got out and gave me a hug then threw my bag into the boot with her bags and guitar. She and her friends were all wearing cotton salwar kameezes. I said hello to the young women, Americans whom I'd met when I'd caught up with Jane on my last trip to Kolkata. They looked happier this time; they were glowing after a few days at the beach, eating fresh fish, relaxing and playing music on the veranda at a hippy hotel. I got the impression they needed an occasional escape.

Jane's flat was a long way from the centre, in the neighbourhood where her husband, Abhik, pastored a church. She may have been middle-class by Indian standards, but her flat was tiny. When I saw her kitchen set-up I inwardly resolved never to complain again about not having enough cooking space.

Jane made us some tea and asked me what had changed at Hebron. It had been years since she had last visited. I gave her news about various mutual friends and confessed that returning to the school always made me a little sad: it had been home to me for so long, but now I knew that I wouldn't be welcome to live there because I wasn't a Christian. It wasn't my place anymore.

'Hey, it's not mine either,' Jane said. Living among Indian people in Kolkata had made her realise that our lives in Ooty had not taught us very much about India. 'We didn't grow up in India; we grew up in Hebron,' she said. We agreed that many of our boarding school classmates, the children of missionaries and aid workers, had probably spent their holidays in something resembling the 'real India'. Almost all of them had spoken at least one Indian language. But she and I had lived in a ghetto. As the children of teachers we had spent the holidays running wild in the almost-deserted school grounds, watching videotaped episodes of *Top of the Pops* or playing on the beach in tourist destinations like Goa and Kovalam. We had learned only a few words of Tamil, and we hadn't needed to use them. Most of what we knew about Indian culture we had learned as adults.

We weren't Indian. But we kept coming back to India.

Jane said she had learned to speak passable Bengali (I think she was being modest). After a few years in Kolkata, she felt that her biggest challenge wasn't the language; it was to live in and understand Indian culture while still keeping hold of her own identity as an Englishwoman. She didn't want the English part of her to disappear. She hadn't come to India to escape being English, and she enjoyed English books and films and television. She was bored with always wearing Indian clothes: 'It's like a uniform,' she said.

A collection of photos of Jane and her family in Gloucester had been stuck to the wall. In one, Jane posed with her mother in the countryside. She wore jeans, a sweater and a scarf. The light was soft, and Jane looked younger, happier, more relaxed. Later, I thought again about Graham: he appeared to have been effortlessly himself, an unreconstructed Queensland bloke wearing walk shorts and long socks, and at the same time he had been completely immersed in the language and culture of his adopted home. Philip, Timothy and Esther had had the same skills, I thought. They had learned early on to switch between their Oriya and Adivasi friends at home and the British culture of Hebron School.

We sat on the couch and drank tea, and I asked Jane about her husband, the pastor. I'd heard the story of their courtship—unusual by British standards for its propriety and by Indian standards for its lack thereof—

and had seen photos of them together on Facebook, both smiling warmly. Abhik was round-faced, short and dark, while Jane was tall, thin and very pale. I wanted to know if she was happy.

Jane smiled. 'People often take me aside and tell me he's a good man,' she said. 'But the Bengali word they use for "good" has lots of deeper connotations about kindness and honesty and integrity.' She said that in the slum community it had caused a stir when she and Abhik had visited and eaten with a poor Bihari migrant family. 'It wasn't so much that a foreigner came to visit; it was that a middle-class Bengali came,' she said. 'People always say to me approvingly that he's not proud.'

Abhik came from a fourth-generation Christian family whose belief had been what Jane described as 'nominal'. He had always loved Jesus, 'what he knew of him', but he had come to a faith of his own in his early thirties. He had founded his own church in a poor area after losing patience with the established, richer churches—the last straw had come when he had taken some slum children to the church 'and people freaked out'.

Abhik was out today, investigating cemeteries after the father of a church family had died unexpectedly a few days earlier. The man had been only in his forties, and it was the first death in the family since they had converted from Hinduism to Christianity. It was also the first death in Abhik's young church. The church community was looking to Abhik to carry out the appropriate ceremony for a Christian death. Abhik didn't think the method of disposing of the body was terribly important, but the man's wife felt very strongly that burial, rather than cremation, was the correct ritual for Christians. She wanted to get this right. Unfortunately, Hindu members of the extended family had forcibly taken the body and had it cremated, though they had returned the ashes to the wife. She, in turn, had passed the ashes on to Abhik, asking him to bury them in the correct Christian fashion. 'Hope it doesn't make you feel weird, but they're in there,' Jane said, gesturing towards the cupboard with her teacup and lowering her voice, even though there was no-one else around.

Jane invited me to visit the slums with her that evening and to sit in on her English lesson and help with the girls' conversation skills. She used the word *busti* to describe the area—she said it was less pejorative than 'slum' and simply described a type of neighbourhood. I wasn't sure what to expect, and I felt a bit odd about going in for a gawk.

Getting across Kolkata that evening took us a couple of hours. We caught two shared autorickshaws through crowded streets, and Jane gave me a very useful piece of advice about making sure my dupatta—the scarf portion of the salwar kameez—wasn't streaming out through the open side of the autorickshaw. 'You don't want to get strangled or dragged off down the street by a motorbike,' she shouted above the engine rattle. I made a horrified face and she laughed. 'It's happened,' she said.

After a local bus trip and then another autorickshaw ride we arrived at the *busti*. The light was beginning to dim. Jane stopped at a roadside stall and bought a packet of biscuits and a bottle of Pepsi to take to the class.

The *busti* contained low-ceilinged concrete rooms joined together in long rows, with narrow lanes running between them. I was reminded of old photos and movie footage of row housing in the industrial north of England, only this was on a smaller scale. The rooms—each one housed a whole family—had small wooden doors with high steps beneath them as protection from flooding during the monsoon. Houses had electricity, but water came from communal pumps in the lanes, and toilets were shared. Some families had lived here for decades and were entrenched tenants who paid little rent.

'Some families are doing quite well,' Jane said. She gestured at a room as we passed. 'The son there just got a job as a security guard in a shopping mall.'

She explained that many of the residents were Hindi-speaking Bihari migrants and children of migrants who had come to the big city looking for work. Many were Muslims, who tended to be poorer and less educated. The struggling families had to live on about six hundred rupees (twelve dollars) a month.

I told Jane about the family who appeared to live on the street corner near my hotel, and I wondered if they would they be moving up to a neighbourhood like this one day. She said there would be several steps in between, which could take years. They were probably very recent migrants, and the men would be doing construction work. The next step for them would be a semi-permanent construction of plastic and bits and bobs somewhere off the street, where they wouldn't get moved on, or at least not as regularly. 'Most of the people who live here have real jobs,' Jane said.

Abhik's church rented a room in the *busti* that was used for classes, health clinics and other services. A huge padlock hung on the wooden door. Jane paused as she pulled out her key to unlock it, like she had something to confess. 'I still feel really uncomfortable coming down here like Lady Bountiful,' she said. She was struggling with having moved out of the *busti* and with being a teacher imparting wisdom instead of just working alongside her neighbours. On the other hand, she said, she knew that these girls would benefit from learning to speak English. Whatever the politics, 'the fact is that job prospects, and therefore general life prospects, are so much better if you can speak English. I've had middle-class Indian people say to me, "What are you teaching slum girls English for? They won't need it." They only see them in one role, and that's as their maidservants.'

The walls of the room were covered with green-painted whitewash flaking around the bottom, no doubt due to monsoon floods. Children's drawings and colour printouts of group photos were stuck to the walls. Bamboo matting had been laid on the concrete floor, and a metal cupboard stood on bricks with a whiteboard leaning against it. The room was not much bigger than my laundry at home. Jane switched on the tube light and ceiling fan.

Two girls who looked about twelve years old came to the door and stood waiting until Jane noticed them and called them in. She spoke with them in Bengali and then explained to me that numbers would be down today because it was exam time for the older girls, and there had been an outbreak of chicken pox in the *busti* so some children were being kept at home.

Jane introduced me to Sita and Poona and told them to ask me some questions.

Very shyly and haltingly they asked 'What is your name?' and 'What is your country?' I asked them some questions in return.

Jane drew a layout of roads and buildings on the whiteboard and labelled them 'cinema hall', 'tea shop', 'my house' and so on. Today, the girls would be learning words like 'next to', 'behind' and 'opposite'.

'Where is the sweet shop?' she asked Sita.

'The … sweet shop is … next to the bank,' Sita replied.

After an hour or so we stopped for a break, and

three older girls joined us. One of them, Soma, was Sita's sister. Jane opened the packet of biscuits and took some metal cups from the cupboard for the Pepsi. Sita and Poona behaved as if Jane and I were guests at their house, pouring our drinks and fussing around us, urging us to have another biscuit.

The girls were all well groomed, wearing clean, pressed salwar kameezes, and they didn't look stereotypically poor to me. I thought again of how little I knew about how most Indian families live. The older girls spoke better English and were more confident in asking me questions. Jane turned their interrogation into the lesson for the evening, making each girl ask and answer questions, and checking that they knew the difference between 'birthday', 'birth date' and 'birth place'. Each girl gave her birth place as 'Chittaranjan Hospital', and they laughed at Jane for pronouncing it incorrectly. 'No, no, Chittaran*jan*,' they insisted.

Jane finished up the class by going over grammatical structure in questions. 'Is it correct to say "Chittaran*jan* Hospital where is it?"' she asked.

The girls all giggled again.

Later, I commented to Jane that it must be hard to stick to correct grammar when it would be much easier to lapse into Indian-English, which is almost a separate dialect.

She sighed and said yes, it was a losing battle most of the time, but she tried to make an effort in English class.

When the class finished Sita and Soma spoke to Jane in Bengali, gesturing towards me. 'They want you to visit their house,' she said. 'I didn't want to take you there like a tourist, but seeing as they've invited you ...'

It was dark outside. Jane locked up the room, and the sisters led us in a complicated route through the alleyways. Doors were open, and light and noise spilled out. Small children ran between the rooms, screaming and playing, chased by women and older children. Jane told me the girls' father would be out, as he worked as a taxi driver. I winced, thinking about all the times I'd haggled with taxi drivers over amounts of money that didn't really mean very much to me. I'd never pictured a taxi driver's family; I had only thought about how they were out to screw as much money from me as they could because I was a foreigner.

The family home was the same size as the room in which the English class was held, with a tube light and ceiling fan. A mezzanine effect had been achieved by making a bed out of boards laid over the tops of two cupboards; the whole family of five slept there, climbing on a stool to reach the bed. Underneath, between the cupboards, was a gas ring for cooking. On a shelf across from the bed a small, fuzzy television played loud Hindi pop music. A calendar on the wall showed a brilliant-blue Krishna, and a fat Ganesh, traditional guardian of the house, was placed over the doorway.

Sita motioned for us to climb onto the bed, where her little brother was playing with marbles. I scrambled up clumsily, determined not to knock anything over or get decapitated by the fan. Jane and I sat cross-legged, and the sisters crawled up next to us, bringing a battered photo album. They wanted to show us their family.

They didn't own a camera, so most of the photos had been taken in studios. A recent brightly coloured picture showed the whole family together in front of a mural of a beach and palm trees. The girls wore matching salwar kameezes, bought especially for the occasion, and everyone looked very solemn. Black-and-white pictures of now-deceased grandparents were shown. In the parents' wedding photo the mother looked about fifteen years old, as young as Soma was now.

Sita wriggled back down onto the stool and then to the ground. She rattled around in the space underneath us and then handed up to me a plastic cup filled with water. 'Take, take,' she said.

Jane and I exchanged the subtlest of concerned looks, which we both knew were about the source of the water.

Sita looked confused for a moment.

I smiled and thanked her and took the suspect water and, for the second time on my journey, drank it.

SKETCH MAP OF
INDIA

English Miles

Darjeeling

10

DARJEELING

When I woke up in my hotel room the next morning, I knew my stomach wasn't right. Downstairs at the bar I skipped my usual chilli-laden omelette and instead ate some toast and drank black tea. I had a ticket in my bag for an upper-bunk berth on an overnight train to Darjeeling. I was due to travel that night, and I felt sick just picturing myself climbing up and down the ladder to my bunk, let alone balancing over a squat toilet as the train swayed from side to side.

I wasn't going to let this thing get in my way. I rested, and in the afternoon I got out my medical kit, consulted my *Health Advice for Australian Travellers* handbook and took a giant dose of antibiotics, a stopper for both ends and some rehydration tablets for good measure. I was going to kill this bug, stomp it dead before it even got started.

It worked pretty well, I have to say. Of course, keeping all the germs corked up inside me meant that my stomach protested by gurgling loudly all night on the Darjeeling Express, but nobody would have been able to hear it over the rumble of the train. In the morning I disembarked at New Jalpaiguri Station, the end of the train line at the foot of the Darjeeling hills. I found myself a hole-in-the-wall shack selling green-chilli omelettes and suffered no ill effects; I sent an email to Chris later in the day with the subject line 'Hurray for Western medicine'.

After I'd eaten I made my way through the station's jeep stand to find a ride up the hill to Darjeeling, and noticed a gaggle of little street urchins following me and laughing.

I smiled at them and kept walking.

The apparent ringleader, a girl who looked to be about ten years old, made a sudden run towards me, hit me hard in the breast and darted off again.

The children all giggled and ran away.

The road up to Darjeeling from New Jalpaiguri reminded me of the road from Coimbatore to Ooty, with the change from tropical to mountainous vegetation, the pot-holed, winding roads, the sudden drops and valley views. The difference is that on this road, the views include rows of jagged, snow-capped mountains appearing from the clouds in the very far distance. Mount Everest—Chomolungma—is across there, somewhere.

Sitting in front of me in the shared jeep on the way up the hill were two blonde British girls who looked about twenty years old. I got chatting to them. Lucy and Sophie were sweet, but completely useless. They were both wearing tank tops and shorts, and they were travelling with enormous, impractical suitcases bursting with Rajasthani bedspreads and carved elephants. I wasn't one to judge: the only reason I didn't have a case full of souvenirs myself was that I'd bought them on previous trips and they already fill my house.

The girls said they were having a great time in India, and they showed me the blotchy skin condition they had picked up along the way.

'This one's getting kind of infected, actually,' Lucy said, lifting her arm to show me a discoloured welt in her armpit.

I suggested that she should perhaps visit a doctor—there was a good clinic in Darjeeling, I assured her—and she looked doubtful. 'I thought I'd just wait till I got home,' she said. 'It's only a couple of weeks.'

I tried not to wince.

Sophie said that the first thing the pair had to do in Darjeeling was find a bank. They had spent their last rupees on a bottle of rum at a shop outside the train station in Kolkata.

'We didn't think we'd sleep that well on the train so we thought it would be funny to get drunk instead,' Lucy said.

I hope I hid my horror. After all, they had survived okay, hadn't they?

Perhaps my face gave me away, because she added, 'It was all fine.'

'Except for that guy,' Sophie said, and the girls giggled.

'Gross!' they both said.

Apparently an Indian man, watching the two scantily clad girls getting drunk together, had been not-too-subtly masturbating under his blanket. I was surprised that was the worst that had happened. I felt motherly towards the two girls, and not in a tender, loving way. More in a way that made me want to give them a good talking to, and possibly a slap, and lock them in their rooms.

When we reached Darjeeling I ended up buying them breakfast; they weren't joking about being out of cash, and the banks weren't open. I directed them to a decent cheap hotel, made them promise to go to a doctor and felt the happy glow of having done a good deed or three.

In retrospect, I'm sure those girls' lives were full of free breakfasts and helpful advice. That's what happens to pretty, useless white girls. I would have been much better off buying breakfast for the street children at New Jalpaiguri Station.

A few months before this trip I had travelled to Darjeeling for the first time, and I had loved it so much that I'd started telling people I was planning to retire there. The cooler weather, the view of the snow-capped Himalayas, the Buddhist influence and the mix of cultures—Nepali, Tibetan, Gurkha, Sikkimese and Bengali—make it the most appealing part of India I have ever experienced.

Of course, Darjeeling's attractions aren't any secret, and the town is full of hotels catering to Indian and foreign tourists. But there is surprisingly little hassle, even in the Kashmiri souvenir shops.

After I booked in to my hotel I wandered the steep, winding streets and ended up in a little shop called the Pompous Tea Emporium on Gandhi Road. I browsed in the half dark, as the power seemed to be out all over Darjeeling, and decided to buy a woollen poncho. I was a bit chilly in my salwar kameez.

An old man who I assumed was Mr Pompous was playing chess on the front stairs. When I waved the poncho at him he came inside and folded it up for me, explaining that this was a traditional Bhutanese costume.

'In Bhutan they call this costume a *poncho*,' he said sagely. He took my money and went back to his chess partner.

A few doors further down I stopped, against all good reason, to pat a fluffy black dog that was sitting in the middle of the street. I missed my dogs at home, and I had noticed that in Darjeeling the dogs are friendlier and healthier and seem to come from far more diverse stock than anywhere else in India. Most other towns have a collection of identical skinny yellow pi-dogs that hang around the rubbish piles, and I have been trained from early childhood to avoid them for fear of the fabled rabies vaccinations that involve ten injections directly into the stomach.

I was staying in a hotel run by an older Tibetan couple, Dawa and Kunzang. They had given me the best room in the house, with a panoramic view across the town and valley and over to the mountains, and the price was suspiciously low. I suspected this was because the owners recognised me from my previous visit, when they had discovered I was researching for Lonely Planet.

'I'm not allowed to take special favours, you know that,' I said.

Kunzang laughed. 'But this time you are not with Lonely Planet, so we can give you anything just because you're our friend,' she said, bringing me another free cup of tea.

Dawa and Kunzang were supporters of the Manjushree Center of Tibetan Culture, an organisation for Tibetan Buddhist refugees living in and around Darjeeling. The centre was set up to keep their culture alive, they told me. I made a note of the discount I was getting at the hotel and decided to donate the difference to the centre when I left.

I spent my evenings in Darjeeling sitting by the old-fashioned wood-burning heater in the common room with Dawa and Kunzang and the other guests, patting their dog and chatting to people about their travels.

One evening a British man shook his head sadly when our hosts were out of the room and said they needed to 'get over it'. 'They're still calling themselves refugees,' he said. 'How can they think that? They've been here since 1959; I don't think they're refugees any more. This is just where they live.'

When Dawa came back I asked him about Tibet. The Tibetan homeland meant everything to him, he told me. He and Kunzang came from families who had escaped Tibet at the same time as the Dalai Lama, during the Tibetan Revolution.

'I was very young when we came, so my memory of Tibet is very dim,' he said. 'We came just after His Holiness the Dalai Lama, with a group. My father was riding a horse and carrying my brother; my mother was riding a yak and carrying me.' Dawa smiled and mimed someone holding reins with one hand and an infant in the other. 'One night when we were sleeping the yak ran away back to Tibet, so after that they found a horse. My parents never expected to live here for fifty years. They left everything as it was, expecting to come back in maybe six months.'

I liked how they assumed the yak had gone back to Tibet. Where else would you want to go?

Dawa's parents were still alive and hoped to return to Tibet one day with their children and grandchildren, 'to relive those glorious days'. The family was still in exile, he said.

Very, very early one morning I got up while the sky was still dark and crept down the stairs and over to the taxi stand, where I caught a shared jeep up to Tiger Hill to watch the sun rise over the Himalayas. I took some photos that suggested I was there alone with only the snow-covered peaks for company. Of course, if I had taken the photos from a few steps further back they would have included scores of tourists from all over India, rugged up in hats and scarves, all trying to photograph the same angle of the morning sun colouring the peak of Kanchendzonga—the third-highest in the world—in shades of pink and orange.

Enterprising Nepali women carried thermos flasks and tiny plastic cups through the crowd, selling ten-rupee shots of sweet, hot coffee and tea. By the time we left, cups littered the ground.

That afternoon I caught the toy train down the mountain just a little way from Darjeeling to the next stop on the line, the tiny settlement of Ghoom. The train rattled past the Druk Sangak Choling Gompa, a big, colourfully painted monastery with flags waving outside and young monks in purple robes running around the courtyard. I was heading for another monastery, the smaller and much older Yiga Choling Gompa in Ghoom.

There were no other visitors at the monastery. I saw a couple of monks, who ignored me. Outside the main building there are rows of prayer wheels set into the front wall. A couple of dogs were snoozing on the ground in front of the wheels. Above the front entrance are four sculpted heads that look like scary, monstrous yaks, or possibly dragons with big teeth. Lotuses are painted around the door.

Inside, the main room is dominated by the gold-coloured Maitreya Buddha, which reaches almost to the ceiling and is draped with scarves. Glass cases along the back wall contain more images of the Buddha. The walls are covered with brilliantly coloured, detailed murals depicting various monsters and demons. A blue demon eats noodles out of a skull while stomping on some naked, puny humans. Next to it, a faded black-and-white photo in a frame shows what looks like a friendly meeting between Pope John Paul II and a young-looking Dalai Lama.

I went back outside and sat on a wooden bench next to a dog, who opened one eye to check me out and then went back to sleep. I might not have felt spiritual, exactly, but I felt very comfortable. I like Buddhists, what I know of them, partly because they have an even more live-and-let-live attitude than Hindus.

The last time I had visited the monastery, sitting out on this bench, I had got talking to an older Tibetan man who had brought a couple of young Americans to visit. I wasn't sure if he had just met them in town or whether they were staying with him. He didn't appear to be a professional tour guide. The Americans were inside looking at the Buddha, and I asked him how he felt about foreigners who wanted to become Buddhists.

The man thought his own religious leader, the Dalai Lama, had the right idea. 'His Holiness says your religion is part of your culture and it's good to stay with your own religion,' he said. 'But if you think you can be a better person, if you believe it's better for you to go to another religion, then go, go; you should be free to do that.'

I looked across at the Himalayas. I have read plenty of criticisms of the Dalai Lama, and I dislike the way he is idolised and misquoted by Westerners who ignore the fact that their hero has supported nuclear-weapons testing and believes that masturbation is a sin. But what the Tibetan man had told me seemed to be very obvious, and simple, and true.

'Live and let live' sounds trite, but it does seem the only way for people to survive together with any real happiness, especially in places where religions co-exist. It's a pity we're all so bad at it.

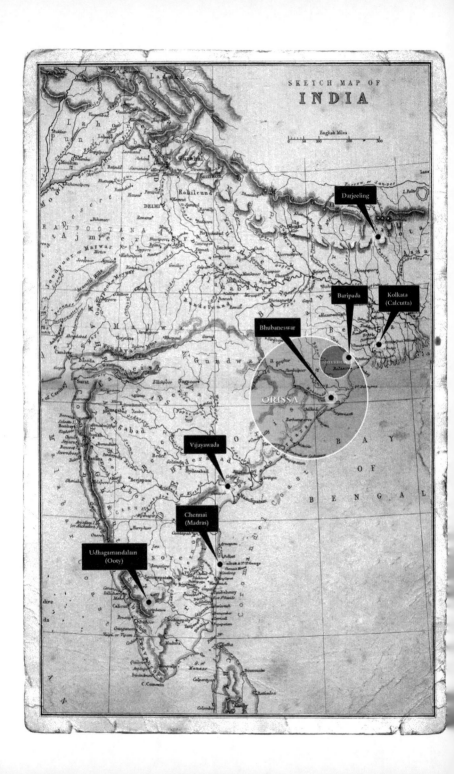

SKETCH MAP OF
INDIA

English Miles

Darjeeling

Baripada

Kolkata
(Calcutta)

Bhubaneswar

ORISSA

Vijayawada

B A Y

O F

B E N G A L

Chennai
(Madras)

Udhagamandalam
(Ooty)

EPILOGUE

I flew home via Singapore. I had told the journalist from the *Hindu* that I'm always happy in Singapore because being there means I'm on my way home, no matter in which direction I'm travelling. I've used this line before, but it isn't just a line. This way of thinking isn't unusual for people who have lived between countries and cultures.

But I returned to Melbourne all the same, like I always do. Chris picked me up at the airport early in the morning and took me back to the place that I call home, mainly because it's where my stuff is. The dogs licked my face and cried with happiness. Of course, they also do that when I come home from a five-minute trip to the milk bar.

I had arrived home to a long, warm autumn. The sky was blue and the light was clear and clean. I walked around the garden sipping from the mug of coffee

that Chris had made for me just the way I like it—black
and bitter—instead of the way I'd been forced to drink
it in India, loaded with milk and sugar. I checked on
the rose bushes that I'd pruned before I left. The dogs
stayed close to me, stopping to piss on the lemon tree;
the blossoms that had covered the tree when I left had
all turned into yellow fruit while I was away.

I called my mother. She said it was good to have
me back and she wanted to see my photos of Ooty. I
promised to email them across. It wasn't easy for her,
knowing that I was going to write about her people, but
she was going to support me all the same.

'Are you up for a trip to the market?' Chris asked
when I hung up the phone.

'Yep,' I said.

I thought about the Australian man I'd met in
Kolkata who was dreaming about the market's doughnut
van from the other side of the ocean. I'd have to eat a
hot jam doughnut or three for him.

No-one was sitting on the ground with a pile of fruit
around them, Indian-style, at the Preston Market, but it
was a lot smellier than a supermarket, or at least it was
where we parked, outside the fish section. We waved at
the Vietnamese woman who sells us our fish, and said
hi to Shane the butcher, and stopped to talk to Pat, the
Italian owner of Placido's Coffee. 'Why you have to go
away?' he said, laughing. 'Preston is the best place in
the world—because I am here!'

Posters around the market advertised its Easter opening hours. A few months earlier, posters wishing people a happy Ramadan had gone up.

We passed the Italian deli that seems to be run by young Indian men, and the stall where Pacific Islanders sell yams, Spam and obscure New Zealand soft drinks, and made our way to the Athena Cafe, where Greek pop videos blare from a television screen.

An old Greek man was smoking out the front and talking to the young waitress. 'I tell you, since I came out in '65, the best one was Gough,' he said to her, punctuating the word 'Gough' with a stab of his cigarette. The waitress nodded and smiled. I don't think she knew who Gough was.

We sat down and ordered a coffee and a souvlaki, and I smiled at Chris. 'I'm not always comfortable identifying myself as an Australian,' I said. 'But I like being a Melbournian.'

Most of the people around me, the shoppers and the traders, had cultural backgrounds that were at least as complicated as mine, and in most cases more so. We have travelled, and continue to travel, sometimes by choice and sometimes not, and we probably all have trouble telling people where we come from. Many of us have left people we love in other parts of the world. But this is where we have landed, and, as places to land go, it seems like a pretty good spot.

Maybe I really am home. Maybe these are my people.

We ate our lunch and chatted with people who stopped to pat the dogs, and then I told Chris I needed to go and have a nap. When we arrived home I looked at the three porcelain tiles that hang on the wall above my desk. I had picked them up for a few dollars at the Coburg Trash and Treasure. They were probably made in the 1950s, and they are painted with scenes from Melbourne: the Shrine of Remembrance, Bourke Street and Yarra Bend. Looking at them, I smiled and thought that I wouldn't trade them for all the Rajasthani bedspreads and elephant carvings in the world.

ACKNOWLEDGEMENTS

I'm very grateful to Gladys Staines for answering questions, checking facts and organising my stay in Baripada.

Thanks to everyone who helped me on the road: Paul and Angie in Ooty, the Gora family in Vijayawada, Subhankar and Mira Ghosh in Baripada, 'Jane and Abhik' in Kolkata and 'Dawa and Kunzang' in Darjeeling.

I'm also indebted to Elisabeth in Perth, Kate Ingleby, Bob Naik and Jyothi Doreswamy for helpful comments, insights and contributions. Bookseller extraordinaire Paul Perry gave me the book's title.

Love and thanks to my partner Chris Gregory for all his help; love and thanks also all my friends and family and especially my very dear parents, Bill and Fran, for their feedback and support and encouragement, even when it wasn't easy for them.

On the publishing front, thanks to Sarah Crisp; you know what you did. At Hardie Grant, thanks go to Fran Berry for her faith in taking me on, Rose Michael for her enthusiasm for and engagement with the text, and Penny Mansley for her considered and thoughtful editing.

REFERENCES

The list below contains details of the books and articles that are quoted from in the text. All Bible quotes are from the New International Version.

ABC Radio National, interview with Gladys Staines, 5 October 2003.

Agnivesh, Swami, article in *Times of India*, quoted in Mangalwadi, Vishal et al., *Burnt Alive*.

Aiyar, Mani Shankar, article in *Sunday* magazine, quoted in Mangalwadi, Vishal et al., *Burnt Alive*.

Banerjee, Ruben, 'In the Land of Dara', *India Today*, September 1999.

Carvalho, Nirmala, '1,793 Christians Reconverted to Hinduism', AsiaNews, 28 April 2008, www.asianews. it/news-en/1,793-Christians-reconverted-to-Hinduism-12119.html.

Denial & Obfuscation: The Report of the Justice DP Wadhwa Commission of Inquiry, South Asia Human Rights Documentation Centre, 30 August 1999, www.hrdc. net/sahrdc/hrfeatures/HRF06.htm.

'Expunge Remarks against Graham Staines', *Hindu*, 23 January 2011.

Gora, *We Become Atheists*, Atheist Centre, Vijayawada, 1975.

'Guided by Instinct', *Hindu*, 14 March 2009.

Heredi, Irene, article in *Times of India*, quoted in Mangalwadi, Vishal et al., *Burnt Alive*.

Mangalwadi, Vishal et al., *Burnt Alive: The Staines Family and the God They Loved*, GLS Publishing, India, 1999.

Parris, Matthew, 'As an Atheist, I Truly Believe Africa Needs God', Times Online, 27 December 2008, www.timesonline.co.uk/tol/comment/columnists/ matthew_parris/article5400568.ece.

Rolley, Ailsa, *Mayurbhanj Messengers*, Evangelical Society in Mayurbhanj, Brisbane, 1996.

Roy, Arundhati, 'Walking with the Comrades', *Outlook*, March 2010.

Roy, Sandip, *The New Colonialism of* 'Eat, Pray, Love', Salon, 13 August 2010, www.salon.com/life/ feature/2010/08/13/i_me_myself.

Rushdie, Salman, 'Outside the Whale', *Granta*, 11, 1984.

Staines, Graham, article in *New Life*, quoted in Rolley, *Mayurbhanj Messengers*.

Venkatesan, J, 'Life Term for Dara Singh Upheld',
    Hindu, 21 January 2011, www.thehindu.com/news/
    national/article1108175.ece.
Zakaria, Fareed, 'How to Restore the American
    Dream', *Time*, October 2010.